NO EXCUSES

NO
EXCUSES

One Man's Incredible Rise Through the NFL
to Head Coach of Notre Dame

CHARLIE WEIS
AND VIC CARUCCI

HarperEntertainment
An Imprint of HarperCollinsPublishers

HarperCollins books may be purchased for educational, business, or sales promotional use. For information please write: Special Markets Department, HarperCollins Publishers, 10 East 53rd Street, New York, NY 10022.

FIRST EDITION

Designed by Laura Kaeppel

Library of Congress Cataloging-in-Publication Data has been applied for.

ISBN-13: 978-0-06-120672-6
ISBN-10: 0-06-120672-5

06 07 08 09 10 WBC/RRD 10 9 8 7 6 5 4 3 2 1

I've been the head football coach at Notre Dame for only one full season, so I surely do not feel as if I have accomplished anything significant yet. When asked to write a book, my answer has always been the same: "Ask me in ten years when I've done something." My wife, Maura, and my son, Charlie, encouraged me to do this in honor of my daughter, Hannah, and all the people with special needs. I dedicate this book to those afflicted with developmental disorders. As a society, we should be more aware of the problems they face in everyday life and show more compassion. Hannah has taught the Weis family many things. She is the reason I humbly agreed to write this book.

CONTENTS

CONTENTS

NO EXCUSES

If You're Going to Have an Opinion, Make Sure It's One That Matters

It's a long way from the student section to the sidelines.

(Courtesy of Michael and Susan Bennett)

> "Notre Dame called last night. . . . I told them they could give you a call."
>
> —Bill Belichick

To this day I am not sure why I dialed the phone. I guess you could blame it on a lot of things, immaturity probably being the biggest. It was a Sunday afternoon in 1975, the day after Notre Dame's football team had lost a game and looked pretty bad doing so. For some reason, I believed that being a student of the university entitled me to issue a complaint about the team's performance. I thought it would be a good idea to take my complaint all the way to the top—to the office of Father Theodore Hesburgh, the school's president at the time.

To be honest, I was fully expecting to get an answering service. I was stunned when Father Hesburgh himself picked up at the other end. It had never dawned on me that he would be done with his Sunday masses and actually sitting in his office at that very moment, ready to answer his phone.

Father Hesburgh was caught off guard as well. He wasn't in the habit of fielding a lot of complaint calls from students. He made me come straight down to his office to tell him exactly what was on my mind.

My passion for sports and thinking that I knew everything there was to know about football—not to mention every other sport—had a lot to do with my being in that situation. When I sat in the stands at Notre Dame, I wasn't just watching the action on the field or on the court. To me, being at the game meant being a part of the game. Our football team won the national championship in 1977, my senior year. Our basketball team went to the Final Four. As a student who went to every game, I felt that I was part of the reason why the University of San Francisco's twenty-nine-game winning streak in basketball came to an end in '77 in our building, the Joyce Center, where the chant was "Twenty-nine . . . and one!" At Notre Dame, the whole student body has always believed it can affect the outcome of a game.

Notre Dame Stadium is like no other place you've ever gone to watch football. Not that there aren't fans everywhere that make a lot of noise, but a game at Notre Dame is something to experience. I still can't believe my eyes when I see, after every Notre Dame score, hundreds of people in the stands doing "air push-ups." That's where they lift people, often recruits who weigh as much as 350 pounds, into the air and do as many push-ups with them as we have points. Or how about fans who crowd surf sixty rows? You just won't find anything like it anywhere else.

But there should be a limit to your enthusiasm, and I had exceeded that limit with my complaint call to Father Hesburgh, who at the time was in his twenty-third year as Notre Dame's president. Father Hesburgh would lead the university for twelve more years until his retirement in 1987. He is considered one of the most influential figures in higher education in the twentieth century.

I walked into his office with my tail between my legs, scared to death that I had gotten myself into trouble. Father Hesburgh had a very intimidating aura. After I nervously shared my point of view on our football team, he basically told me that I didn't get a vote. What I thought about the football team wasn't important, he said; I should go back and be a good student who was loyal to the school and its teams, and not consider my opinion one that mattered.

Fortunately, the stern lecture was the extent of my punishment. But that didn't make it any less painful. I remember walking out of that office feeling as humbled as you could possibly be.

Now flash forward nearly thirty years, to early December 2004. Once again I was on the phone with a member of the administration at the University of Notre Dame. This time I was on the receiving end of the call, at my office in Gillette Stadium in Foxboro, Massachusetts, home of the New England Patriots.

I was going about my usual business as the Patriots' offensive coordinator, trying to help them win their third Super Bowl in four seasons. John Heisler, Notre Dame's senior associate athletics director, was asking whether I would be interested in speaking with Kevin White, the school's director of athletics, about replacing Tyrone Willingham, who had just been fired as head coach.

Imagine that. The opinionated fan who used to sit in the student section had an opinion about Notre Dame football that just might matter after all. It brought a sarcastic smile to my face.

I told John that protocol would be for Kevin to call Bill Belichick, the Patriots' head coach, to ask for permission to talk with me. Belichick got that call on Saturday night, December 4, while we were in Cleveland getting ready for our game the next day against the Browns. I was anxious to hear about what had transpired in the conversation between Bill and Kevin, but that wouldn't happen until Sunday morning, during our pregame meal, when Bill came up to me and said, "Notre Dame called last night. . . . I told them they could give you a call." Not that I was expecting him to tell me otherwise, but still it was a relief to hear that he had given his official blessing.

We beat the Browns, 42–15. On Tuesday morning, as we began game planning for our next opponent, Cincinnati, Kevin called to say he wanted to come to New England to interview me.

"When do you want to do that?" I asked.

"Today," he said.

"Great."

"When are you available?"

"Any time after midnight."

"Excuse me?"

"Any time after midnight."

I had made a commitment to Belichick that I would not let the pursuit of the Notre Dame job, or any head-coaching position for that matter, distract me from my work with the Patriots. I would spend all day and all night working on the offensive game plan, as I always did on Tuesday before a Sunday game, and midnight was when I usually finished. If Kevin wanted to interview me on Tuesday, that was the time I would be available.

"Okay," he said.

The meeting was set for 12:30 A.M., at the Westin Hotel in Providence. I knew I wasn't going to feel the least bit spent. Are you kidding me? I was already operating on adrenaline because of our playoff run, and now we're talking about the chance to coach football at Notre Dame, the premier football program in the country.

I had gone to school there. I'm a Catholic. Ask college football fans anywhere to name the one program they would want to run, and probably more than half are going to say Notre Dame. This wasn't just any job.

THE PREVIOUS SUMMER, during training camp, Belichick and I had spoken about head-coaching opportunities in college football, after I'd been a candidate for two NFL head-coaching positions, with the Buffalo Bills and the New York Giants, and missed out on both of them in part because of the Patriots' success. Our playoff runs would allow an NFL team to interview me only once, during a designated time frame, but I could not be offered a job until our season was over. Otherwise, the team making the offer could be accused of tampering and if found guilty could end up forfeiting multiple draft picks. That's a price no team wants to pay if it doesn't have to.

The Bills and Giants didn't want to wait; they went with coaches who were immediately available to be hired—Mike Mularkey went to Buffalo, and Tom Coughlin to the Giants. Some NFL teams feel the longer they wait, the harder it is to find good assistant coaches for the head coach to put his program in place. It's different with colleges. Because they are not in direct competition with NFL teams, there are no restrictions on when or how often they can make contact with NFL assistants, and they don't have to wait until after the season to hire them.

I wasn't pessimistic about my prospects of becoming an NFL head coach, but I had started doing some research on these college jobs, which were starting to pay pretty well. The guys taking them were getting long-term contracts, and they seemed happy.

"I think I ought to at least explore a couple of these jobs if they come open," I said to Bill.

"Which ones?"

"Notre Dame and South Carolina."

Notre Dame I've already explained. I was interested in South Carolina because my wife, Maura, and I plan to retire there.

By chance, both jobs came open at the same time.

My agent, Bob LaMonte, had already been preparing me to interview for NFL head-coaching positions. Bob, who is based in Reno, Nevada, specializes in representing football coaches, and he is good enough at it that he usually doesn't have to go after clients. They come to him. Two of his coaches who are friends of mine, Andy Reid of the Philadelphia Eagles and John Fox of the Carolina Panthers, had told him that he should represent me.

Bob gives you a whole book to study on the interview process, then goes over all of the material with you. He believes that within the first ten minutes you have to be able to tell people conducting the interview who you are, what made you who you are, and what you stand for. Bob put me through hours and hours of mock interviews. After that, I felt well schooled going into an interview. I was ready.

When you're clearly "the guy" for a head-coaching job in football, you're clearly "the guy." When you're part of a pack, one of three or four candidates, and the people doing the hiring don't have any preconceived notion of who's getting the job, a good interview is what separates you from the rest.

I believe that if you have the goods to become a head coach you should be able to avoid a poor interview. If you don't interview well, chances are you didn't prepare, and if you don't prepare, you don't have the goods. You'd better be prepared, because you're going to be in charge of an organization. Among many other attributes, you need to have people skills, and you need to demonstrate that you can run the show. These abilities are evident in an interview.

That summer, I also prepared in case the right college job came open, because once the NFL season starts, you don't have time to study colleges or anything else; you're totally involved in the season. So I did some research on how I'd put a college staff together. At that point, I had been in the pros for fourteen years already, and most of the guys I knew didn't want to go back to the college level. I came up with a thought process on putting together a staff based more on a concept than on targeting specific people to hire.

Relationships between the coaches would be important because building a cohesive staff was imperative. I wanted, on both sides of the ball, at least two guys who had worked together at some point so that there was some kind of rapport already established. In addition to that, even if I couldn't hire people from the Patriots, I wanted to have some familiarity with the coaching of the people I did hire. I also wanted some alumni on the staff, people who would understand the school's traditions and bring the sense of pride that helps make any football program successful. Last but not least, I wanted people with recruiting-coordinator backgrounds because I felt that coming from the NFL, that would be one area where I would have the most catching up to do.

A couple of my boys from the University of South Carolina, where I had gotten my first taste of big-time football as a graduate assistant and served in other coaching and recruiting capacities, called to tell me that it looked like Steve Spurrier was going to be the guy there. They wondered whether I wanted to get my name into the mix.

"Hell, no, I don't want to get my name into the mix," I said. "Why would I want to do that only to lose out to Spurrier?"

KEVIN WHITE AND Father John Jenkins, Notre Dame's president, flew to Providence on a private plane (owned by Jim Morse, a Notre Dame alumnus), in order to prevent anyone tracking the flights of the Notre Dame–owned planes, which can be done easily through the Internet if you have the tail numbers. Once someone saw that a Notre Dame plane was on a midnight flight to Providence, it wouldn't be a reach to assume that the trip probably involved a meeting with yours truly. In a matter of seconds, that information would be all over the Web like a rash.

Early in our conversation, I told Kevin and Father Jenkins that I was not leaving the Patriots until the season was over. If that was going to be a deal breaker, it was important for them to know that up front.

"I've already talked with Bill Belichick," I said. "Bill would go out of his way to work with me if I were to get the job now and then move out there after we finish playing. I am not going to sacrifice the Patriots' season just to get this job."

After that, I gave them about a ten-minute spiel about my personal makeup. I talked about who I was and what I stood for, and the people who got me where I was at that point. I talked about the very first major influence on my coaching career, John Chironna, the head coach at Morristown High School in New Jersey. I talked about the late Joe Morrison, who gave me one of the biggest breaks of my career when he hired me at South Carolina. I talked about Bill Parcells, who gave me my first coaching job in the NFL with the Giants. And, of course, I talked about Bill Belichick.

I emphasized both Parcells and Belichick because they were the critical players in shaping me as a coach, and they would be my two biggest references.

A significant part of the discussion focused on being a graduate of Notre Dame, which had been the case with only two Fighting Irish coaches in the previous forty-two years. I thought that anyone who had gone to school there would have a huge advantage over somebody who hadn't. Urban Meyer, the coach at Utah and a former assistant at Notre Dame, was rumored to have been offered the position, but he later accepted the head-coaching job at Florida.

Now, Notre Dame was talking with only three guys, all who had university connections: Greg Blache, a former defensive back and assistant coach at Notre Dame who was coaching with the Washington Redskins; Tommy Clements, a former quarterback and assistant coach at Notre Dame who was the offensive coordinator for Buffalo; and me. They knew Blache and Clements because they had coached and played there. They didn't know me.

How much did people really know about any of the coaches on the Patriots' staff? You'd know who we were, but you wouldn't know us, because Belichick, like Parcells, rarely allowed assistant coaches to speak with the media.

I think Kevin and Father Jenkins liked the combination of my football background and what I was about as a person. People can read your bio in the media guide to find out about everything you've done as a football coach, but until they talk with you they don't know about you as a person. When they started hearing about how important my family is and about my special-needs daughter, Hannah, and about my son, Charlie, who's my best buddy, and about how my wife is my closest friend, they got a much more complete picture.

Early in the interview I knew where this was going. I could tell by the questions, and by the look on their faces as I answered. I wasn't sure, but I felt very good about my chances.

I thought this would be a perfect way for me to walk away from the NFL. Two previous jobs for which I had been rumored were in the AFC East. One, which came after the 2003 season, was with the Bills. The other, which came up during the '04 season, was with the Miami Dolphins. I'm not saying the Dolphins ever considered hiring me over the guy they did hire, Nick Saban, but there was a point when my name was attached to that job. Either way, I felt too good about my relationship with New England to want to go somewhere and be a direct adversary.

WHEN THE INTERVIEW ended, at about three thirty in the morning, I still had that adrenaline rush going. I went home and spoke with Maura for a few minutes because she was anxious to hear what had happened. Then I slept for about an hour, got up, and went to work.

On Friday, December 10, Kevin White called to ask if I would take part in a conference call so that a group of players on the Notre Dame football team could interview me. That was fine. Among the members of the group were quarterback Brady Quinn, linebacker Brandon Hoyte, and defensive lineman Victor Abiamiri. They were college kids. What were they going to ask that I couldn't answer? The interview lasted maybe a half hour. Although they were reading from a prepared list of questions, I could feel that they were a little intimidated.

At about eight o'clock that night, as I sat at the kitchen table in our home with Maura and Charlie, who was eleven at the time, I received another call from Kevin. He said he was faxing me a two-page proposal for a six-year contract that would run from 2005 through 2010. My wife and I had set some financial parameters, based on the confidence that my shot at an NFL head-coaching job wasn't too far down the road. If the Notre Dame offer fell short of our number, we were just going to say, "No, thank you." We were not even going to negotiate. If the offer met our number, then we would negotiate. If the number was greater than our number, then we had a deal.

I was still on the phone with Kevin when the fax machine in our office rang. Maura walked into the office, then back into the kitchen. She was holding the fax, and had a big smile on her face and tears in her eyes. She gave me a thumbs-up. I'm not going to reveal the number, but let's just say it was better than I was expecting. It was so good, in fact, that the only additional money I sought was so I could hire top-notch assistant coaches. As a career assistant in the NFL, I always appreciated the importance of surrounding yourself with a good staff. Notre Dame came through on that count as well.

When I told Belichick that I had accepted the offer, he was happy for me. At the same time, he was concerned that the news of my heading to Notre Dame after the season would be a distraction, which was the main reason that the Patriots said nothing publicly about it right away even though the word was on the street. I wasn't supposed to say a word to anyone on the team, and I didn't. Of course, there are different ways to communicate besides using words. On Saturday morning, before going through final preparations for the game, Tom Brady, our quarterback and one of the select few players I have coached that I ever allowed myself to call a friend, walked up to me. He didn't speak. He just held his arms apart with his palms up, as if to say, "Well?"

I just gave him a look. Maybe I had a little smile on my face. I didn't say anything, but Tommy knew. He gave me a big hug. He was pumped. He wasn't pumped that I was leaving. He was just pumped for me.

Right after our 35–28 home victory over the Bengals, Bill told the team that I had accepted the offer from Notre Dame and would be leaving after the season. A bunch of the players came up to say that they were happy for me. Robert Kraft, the Patriots' chairman and CEO, was happy for me too. Until word got around that I had taken the Notre Dame job, he said, he hadn't realized how many friends he had in business who graduated from there. "There are Notre Dame people all over the place!" he said.

Notre Dame had a private jet waiting after the game to take me to South Bend, along with Maura and Charlie. A police escort got us right out of that impossible postgame traffic snarl that you always get in Foxboro, and it was smooth sailing all the way to the airport.

The news conference introducing me as the new head football coach wasn't scheduled until the next day, but I addressed the players that night at the Joyce Center, where the football offices and meeting rooms were before they moved to the newly constructed, $22 million Guglielmino Athletics Complex. The players were all in their seats when I arrived. They were quiet, not knowing what to expect from me.

There were too many other people besides the players in the meeting room—administrators, sports-information people, trainers—for me to say what I really wanted to say. What I did say was this: They were 6–5 at the time, and as much as some of them might have wanted to believe they were better than that and talk about games they "could have" or "should have" won, that was what they were—a 6–5 team. "Could have" and "should have" don't mean a thing. Using a favorite line of Parcells, I told them, "You are what your record says you are."

A couple of months later, when it was only the players and me, I gave them the unedited version. There had been some discussion around the campus and in the media that Willingham, who went on to become head coach at the University of Washington, had gotten a raw deal with his firing. It got back to me that a bunch of the players felt that way too.

My unedited comments, with some choice adjectives thrown in that I won't repeat in this book, went like this: "Quit blaming everyone but yourselves for the coaching change. There was a coaching change because you're 6–6, and last year you were 5–7. There was a coaching change because you guys didn't live up to expectations around Notre Dame. You guys are sitting here, bitching and moaning about the administration for the coaching change. I tell you what, go 5–7 and 6–6 the next two years and you'll get rid of me, too.

"So just shut the hell up. Why don't you just look in the mirror? Maybe the reason you've gone 5–7 and 6–6 is that you've played crummy. Just maybe."

Rest assured, I had their full attention. You could have heard a pin drop. They received my message loud and clear: "No excuses!"

Before the news conference the next day I walked, with my wife and son, into what would serve as my temporary office while the new one was being finished. There was a poster on the wall with a montage of pictures of Knute Rockne, Frank Leahy, Ara

Parseghian, Dan Devine, and Lou Holtz. Of all of the coaches in the long and rich history of Notre Dame football, only those five faces were up there.

I looked at Charlie and said, "You know what success is?"

"What?" he said.

"Success is if ten or fifteen years from now, when I leave, they put another face on that poster—mine. It will mean that I handled myself with class. I ran the program with integrity. I brought in kids who could read and write and who graduated from college. And it will mean that we won a whole bunch of football games. To be a success at Notre Dame, you can't have one, two, or three of those things. You have to have all four."

I won't settle for anything less than that.

2

From the Middle of Jersey to Middle America, the Next Marv Albert Chases His Dream

In our neighborhood, it was all sports, all the time.

(Courtesy of the author)

> "Why won't they run the ball? . . . Why aren't
> they throwing? . . . Why not blitz here?"

> —Charlie Weis, Notre Dame student
> and aspiring broadcaster

'm a Jersey guy, which means I can tell the difference between someone who really is from New Jersey and someone who claims to be but really isn't. Here's how: If you ever call anyone from Jersey and he has an 856 or 609 area code, he's from part of Pennsylvania, not from New Jersey. You need a 201, 732, 908, or 973 area code to say you live in New Jersey. Just kidding!

It's like the Mason-Dixon Line. There's a dead spot in the state, a spot where everyone turns into a Sixers, Flyers, Eagles, and Phillies fan, instead of a Knicks, Rangers, Giants, and Yankees or Mets fan. My pro teams have always been the Knicks, Rangers, Giants, and Yankees.

I've lived in a bunch of places, and this is what I like the most about the people of New Jersey: They don't trust very many people, but once you earn somebody's trust, you're friends for life. You might not have as many friends as someone else, but your friendships are not superficial. For me it's still the same eight guys that I was hanging out with in high school, and in one case all the way back to kindergarten. We're all married. Most of us have kids. To this day, on one Saturday every summer, we get together at Monmouth Park to bet the ponies. We even sit on the same benches we sat on when we were eighteen, except for 2006, when we moved to the clubhouse, where Maura threw me a surprise fiftieth-birthday party.

I was born in Trenton, but I don't remember anything about living there. My dad, also named Charlie, was just out of the navy and attending Rider College, which was in Trenton at the time before it moved to Lawrenceville. My mother, Debbie, was working as a nurse to put him through school. She spent most of her time working in intensive care. With two of the eventual five kids to care for—I have an older sister and three younger brothers—she normally worked from 11 P.M. to 7 A.M. in order to be home during the day.

After college my father went to work as an accountant. He spent most of his time working for Lockheed Electronics, which later became Lockheed Martin, the world's largest military contractor. He was an excellent athlete. He grew up in Port Jervis, New York, and to this day there are people who say that he was one of the greatest athletes to come out of that area. He played all sports, but he made his name playing baseball. My dad was talented enough to have an opportunity to play for the St. Louis Cardinals out of high school, but he joined the navy. He was on the first boat to reach Hiroshima in 1946, a year after the atomic bomb was dropped there to end World War II.

I have a niece who once dated a guy who was a pitcher in the minor leagues. One day she introduced him to me, and he was more excited to meet the son of Charlie Weis than he was to meet Coach Charlie Weis.

When I was five, we moved to Middlesex, a middle-class town in the heart of central New Jersey. My parents always believed the easiest way to keep an eye on your kids was to encourage them to be around the house rather than discourage them from doing so. In summertime, we'd spend many days in our backyard playing Wiffleball and then cooling off in our aboveground pool. Among the rules we had were that if you hit the ball in the pool or over the fence in left field, it was an automatic home run, even though half the pool was in foul territory. However, if you hit the ball over the right-field fence, it was an out because you couldn't get to the ball without climbing over other people's fences. You always tried to punch it into the pool, which was about seventy feet from home plate. This was back when Wiffleballs were solid on one half and had holes in the other half, which allowed you to throw curve-balls, screwballs, risers, and sinkers. Now, there are holes throughout the ball.

Our Wiffleball games ranged from two-on-two to six-on-six. I had three younger brothers who liked to play, and we also had a lot of friends and other kids from the neighborhood over. My friends and I all lived within a mile of each other. Just about anywhere you needed to go you could get to by hopping on your bike. And when you got there, you were usually playing a sport. As soon as you finished one game, it would be "Saturday morning, see you at the basketball courts at nine." You'd show up and everyone would be there. During baseball season it was "See you at the field at nine."

We played street hockey in front of the house or in the parking lot of a nearby bank—after hours and on weekends—because the curbs kept the little red rubber ball that we used as a puck in play. Or we took our sticks, with the hard plastic blades and the wooden shafts, and our nets and played in our basement. The area was small, so we ended up whacking each other more than we did that little ball. When we played hoops, we'd lower the basket so everyone could dunk.

I've always loved sports. I can't think of a day in my whole life that hasn't included playing, watching, thinking about, or talking about sports in one form or another.

The first sport that I truly embraced as a kid was baseball because it was the only one I was good at—good enough, at least, to play on an organized basis. My father and the principal of my junior high school were the coaches for all of my four years in Little League. How's that for a combination of authority figures to keep you in line? If there were going to be any problems with behavior on that team, they certainly weren't going to come from me.

I was always big and chunky, so hoops were never an option. I couldn't play Pop Warner football because I was over the weight limit. That meant I never played organized football until I got to high school, and once I did I was way behind.

On top of that, I developed Osgood-Schlatter disease, which causes calcium deposits to form in your knees and you get swelling. It's common among active children between the ages of ten and fifteen, and I had it bad my sophomore year. I wasn't all that athletic to start off with, and the disease narrowed things for me even further. My senior year I was on the varsity football team as a backup center, and didn't play very much. In addition, I played Catholic Youth Organization (CYO) basketball.

The one experience that helped the most to build my coaching philosophy came in my senior year of high school. We had only fifteen uniforms for our varsity baseball team, which meant that that was how many players would be picked from the tryouts. I was one of the fifteen.

After two games five guys quit over a lack of playing time, leaving us very thin to say the least. Our coach, Kevin Donovan, talked with the ten of us who were left about how he planned to handle the situation. He could have brought back some of the guys that he had cut. He could have brought up some guys from junior varsity. He did neither. He decided instead that we were going to play the rest of the season with ten guys.

You want to talk about having to work together as a team! There were four pitchers that all played other positions. I was the catcher. If I wasn't at bat, I was usually warming up a pitcher who was going to be playing shortstop, third base, second base, or somewhere in the outfield. We could never have anyone warming up in the bullpen because every pitcher we had was already playing another position.

It was probably the best sports experience I ever had because it helped me understand how everyone's got to count on everybody else. You never had to worry about whether or not you were playing. You could count on your name being on that lineup card every game. You knew that you had to show up or else you'd be letting down the entire team.

As a catcher I was knocked around a bit and banged up some, but I never missed a game. You didn't even entertain the thought. When I think back to all of those lessons that I learned from Bill Parcells and Bill Belichick about putting the team first, lessons that were ingrained in me throughout my coaching career, I am

always reminded of that baseball season. You couldn't get any
more of a team concept than that.

What made it carry even more weight with the ten of us on that
team was the fact that we ended up winning most of our games. It
was like the movie *Hoosiers,* where the players come to realize that
the only way they're going to succeed is by relying on each other
all of the time—and they do.

OTHER THAN SPORTS, some of the best memories from my
youth go back to the time I spent at the Jersey Shore. I've loved
everything about the Shore since the first of many trips our family made there when I was a kid. I continued to go on my own
through high school and college (before eventually living there on
two separate occasions as an adult).

It was a big social gathering. You just enjoyed hanging on the
beach. Your choice of beach would be determined by your age. As
a kid, you went to the "family" beaches. If you were in high school,
Seaside Heights was the place to go. Just as there are different
types of beaches, there are also different types of boardwalks.
The Seaside Heights boardwalk is about four miles long and has
wheels of fortune and all sorts of games of chance, whereas the
Point Pleasant boardwalk has rides and other attractions geared
more toward younger kids.

The Shore was only forty-five minutes away by car. It took a lot
longer to get there by bicycle, but before I had my driver's license
that was the only means of transportation my buddies and I had
when we decided, as teenagers, to make a trip on our own to Seaside Heights. An uncle and aunt of one of the guys invited us to
spend a few days at their bed-and-breakfast in Seaside Park, so a

half dozen of us hopped on our bicycles early on a Saturday night and headed for the Shore. We tried to avoid the major roads—and the obvious danger that went with traveling them on bikes—as best we could. I remember going through New Brunswick and then heading down Route 18. Eventually, we had to get on some major roads, but we made it.

Getting there was an adventure, which made it fun. Coming back? That was miserable. It seemed like it took an eternity. Going down, you had the excitement of actually getting there. Coming back, it wasn't nearly the same. Our parents didn't have any problem with us going to the Shore. Of course, we didn't necessarily say we were going on bicycles. I know I wouldn't let my son make a journey like that. Not in a million years.

The Jersey Shore season goes from Memorial Day to Labor Day. That's when all of the tourists, known as "Bennies," are there. There are different explanations for the origin of the term "Benny," which goes all the way back to the beginning of the twentieth century. One is that it's an acronym for where most of the tourists come from: Bergen, Essex, Newark, and New York. Another is that it came from the fact that some of the luggage of tourists arriving at the Shore would be marked "BEN E" for eastbound trains from Bensonhurst. Still another is that it was short for "beneficial rays," which was what all of those pale tourists planned to get by spending a summer at the Shore.

When we made those trips down there as kids and teenagers, we were Bennies. Starting when I was a senior in high school, I'd get together with a bunch of guys and we would rent a place on the Shore for the summer. Back then, you could get a place for five thousand dollars for the summer, which wasn't too bad when you had ten guys to put in five hundred bucks apiece. We'd cook out, swim in the ocean day and night, go to clubs . . . just have a good time. It was worth every penny.

When we lived at the Shore, we were locals, aka "Clam Diggers." The locals have never been too happy to have the Bennies around, mainly because of all of the traffic jams and crowdedness that they bring. When you're a local, the best time at the Shore is after Labor Day because that's when all of the Bennies leave. Now, the beach is yours again. The boardwalk's yours again. The restaurants are yours again.

GROWING UP IN Middlesex you were either a Yankee or a Met fan. I was a Yankee fan. Almost everyone in that area rooted for the Giants; hardly anyone rooted for the Jets. You rooted for the Knicks; the Nets were not even in New Jersey at the time. You rooted for the Rangers; the Devils were the Colorado Rockies at the time.

And you rooted for your teams with passion.

My father took me to my first Yankee game when I was six or seven years old, but I don't remember much about it. I do remember watching the New York football Giants play in Yankee Stadium, because we sat in the left-center-field bleachers, which were behind one of the end zones. As we got into our early teens, a bunch of friends and I used to make five to ten trips each summer to New York to watch the Yankees play. We weren't old enough to drive, so we'd take the bus from the center of Middlesex to the Port Authority in New York City. From there, we'd take the subway to Yankee Stadium. You got on the A train to 59th Street and then you got on the D train to 161st. One guy, Freddy Herzog, would order eight hot dogs as soon as he got to the stadium, then sit there and eat all eight hot dogs himself. We used to like to go when there were twinight doubleheaders, which Major League Baseball would play back then to make up rainouts. The first game would start at five o'clock, and we'd stay until the sixth or seventh inning of the second game, so we'd be there a whole evening.

When the Knicks and Rangers were on the road, I watched their games on TV, WOR, channel 9. None of their home games were telecast, so you listened to Marv Albert, who did the Knicks and Rangers games. The more I listened, the more I knew what I wanted to be—a sports announcer, like Marv Albert. I liked Marty Glickman, who did the Giants games. I liked Mel Allen, Red Barber, and Phil Rizzuto on the Yankee broadcasts.

My favorite, though, was Marv Albert because he could announce a game on the radio and I could envision what was actually happening. That's why I thought he was phenomenal. If it was the Knicks, you always knew how the guards were dribbling or where the ball was going. *"Frazier over to Monroe . . . DeBusschere from the corner . . . Yes! It counts and he's fouled!"* If it was the Rangers, you knew who could handle the puck, who fanned on the shot. *"Stick save and a beauty made by Giacomin!"* I can still hear him making those calls.

I followed all the action on my little transistor radio in my bedroom upstairs, usually with the earpiece in so my parents wouldn't know I was still up late at night. That came in especially handy when the Yankees were on the West Coast and the games didn't start until eleven o'clock. I was as much a fan of the broadcasts as I was of the teams. I loved Mickey Mantle, but I remember Mel Allen, too. *"Hello, there, everybody! This is Mel Allen. . . ."*

Around my junior year of high school I decided that I wanted to go into broadcasting. I realized I wasn't a very good athlete. I knew I wasn't going to play in the major leagues. I might have been able to play sports through my senior year of high school, and even go to some small college and be a participant, but the major leagues? They were out of the question. Still, I loved sports too much to not be involved with them after high school.

So what are your choices? Writing or broadcasting. You have coaching, too, but that wasn't even a thought in my mind at that time. I was a talker, and I thought that I was good at it. I thought that I was smart. I thought I knew sports. I figured it would be the perfect way for me to go.

I started looking into colleges that had a communications department and had major sports teams that you could follow. I didn't want a school with fewer than five thousand students, but I didn't want one with more than ten thousand, either. I wanted to go to a good university where I'd be a name, not just a number. Back then, we actually had a computer in our guidance department that you could feed with your interests in order of priority, and it would fire out schools that matched. Notre Dame was the first one that came out.

I'm a Catholic, but I didn't grow up saying, "I want to go to Notre Dame." I wasn't a guy who woke up singing, "Cheer, cheer, for old Notre Dame!" I did like Notre Dame just from watching the Sunday morning football highlights on television, with Lindsey Nelson, who also used to be the voice of the Mets, saying, "Now we'll move to further action late in the third quarter. . . ." That was what intrigued you. You had no idea where South Bend, Indiana, was, but if someone asked you where Notre Dame was, you knew it was in South Bend strictly from watching those highlights (even though, technically, it's not in South Bend; it's in Notre Dame, Indiana).

I applied to Notre Dame and some other schools and was accepted at all of them. I picked Notre Dame because I thought it was the best fit. Relatively speaking, it wasn't that expensive—tuition, room, board, books, and fees in my freshman year came to about thirty-five hundred dollars. In order to get a communications degree, I had to major in speech and drama, which was part of the College of Arts and Letters.

The first visit I made to the campus was when I walked in the door for my freshman year in 1974. The first question I had was "Where's the sun?" For about a month, I didn't see it. I was homesick, too, but eventually the sun did come out and everything seemed better.

I didn't appreciate the history and tradition of Notre Dame until I got there. Most students and alumni feel them on game day. It's something I can't describe. It's like trying to describe that "it" that you find in all of the good quarterbacks. You just know when you're around it—or when it's around you.

There's an aura about the place, and it takes hold of you when you see the Golden Dome . . . Touchdown Jesus . . . Notre Dame Stadium . . . the Grotto of Our Lady of Lourdes, where people go and pray. There are people who come to Notre Dame just to go to the Grotto with all of the candles and St. Joseph's Lake in the background. It's the second-most visited place in the state of Indiana after the Brickyard, the site of the Indianapolis 500.

I WENT TO all of the football games at Notre Dame; Ara Parseghian was the head coach my freshman year, and Dan Devine was the head coach for the last three years. I went to all of the basketball games. I went to hockey games. I went to baseball games. That was my way of being part of the experience.

Your seats in the student section for football and basketball games get a little better during each of your four years of enrollment. For football games you start out in the end zone as a freshman, and each year you move one section over until you end up at around the 30-yard line as a senior.

When I was in the stands, I was always accused of "broadcasting" the game. I would have a running commentary going. I would yell things like "Why won't they run the ball? . . . Why aren't they throwing? . . . Why not blitz here?" I was the ultimate armchair quarterback. My friends who were sitting with me never told me to shut up. They probably wanted to, and I wouldn't have blamed them if they had, but they didn't, because they usually thought that I knew what I was talking about.

The first two football players that I was affiliated with were Terry Eurick, a running back, and Terry Murphy, a center. They were both from Saginaw, Michigan. We started school together on the second floor, section 2B, of Flanner Hall, and we ended four years later on the same floor, same section, of Flanner (which is now an administration building). They were my boys—two of the eight or ten of us who were friends all through college, just like my boys from Jersey.

It has been widely reported that I was a roommate of Joe Montana. Not true. We were friends, but never roommates. First, Joe lived in another dorm. Second, he got married freshman year. From the time he was a freshman until his senior year, he was living with his wife off campus. He was close friends with Eurick, so that was where our relationship started. Because our dorm was right next to the Stepan Center, where the Friday night football pep rallies were held back then, Joe would stop by on the way to the rally. He did not act like a prima donna. To me he was just a good guy I went to school with who played football.

What I remember most about Joe from school was that he was one of the most phenomenal all-around athletes I've ever seen. A lot of people don't know that, because they know him only as a football player. You should have seen him play hoops.

Joe was a fierce competitor, and where that would show up even more than on the football field was in the pickup basketball games we had. He had about a forty-inch vertical jump back then (he has about a six-inch vertical jump now). He was one of the best basketball players on campus. Joe and Digger Phelps, Notre Dame's basketball coach at the time, had conversations, and Joe almost split from football to basketball when he wasn't getting much playing time on the football team.

Here's what most people don't know about Montana: at the beginning of his fourth year at Notre Dame, he was the third-team quarterback. Not the second. Not the first. The third. In the third game of the year, we were playing Purdue. The starting quarterback, Rusty Lisch, struggled and was pulled. The second guy, Gary Forystek, took a hard hit that knocked him out and broke his clavicle.

Rather than putting Joe in the game, Dan Devine went back to Lisch. Finally, with two minutes left in the third quarter and Purdue leading, 24–14, Montana came in. He ended up rallying us to seventeen points in the fourth quarter, and we won. Joe was the starter for the rest of the season.

We went on to beat Texas, 38–10, to win the national championship. Not that Joe needed to do much. Our offensive line took control of the game, allowing two of our running backs, Jerome Heavens and Vegas Ferguson, to run for a hundred yards. Terry Eurick had two touchdowns on his first two touches! Our defense, led by Bob Golic, manhandled a Texas offense that featured Earl Campbell.

The following year, his fifth season, Joe played in that famous "Ice Bowl" Cotton Bowl against Houston, when he overcame an ice storm, minus-ten wind chill, and the flu to lead us back from twenty-two points down to win the game on the last play. Think about it. At halftime he was in the locker room, shaking uncontrollably because his body temperature had dropped to ninety-six degrees. He was covered with blankets and coats and drinking all of the chicken soup he could swallow. Then, in the second half, he gave one of the great performances in college football history.

Joe was able to be a third-round draft choice in the NFL because he was one of the first fifth-year guys Notre Dame ever had. Almost everyone there graduates in four years, but because of a shoulder separation he suffered in his junior year, Joe stuck around for an extra year, allowing him to play in back-to-back Cotton Bowls.

To me Joe was always normal. His stardom didn't truly take hold until he got to the NFL with San Francisco. He became more of a star at Notre Dame after he left. He became Joe Montana, the Legend, by winning those four Super Bowls and being a three-time Super Bowl MVP with San Francisco.

EURICK, MURPHY, AND the rest of us argued a lot, as all friends do. We'd argue about all sports. We'd argue about music. We'd argue about everything. I always thought I was right, but I knew that I was just one of many guys on campus who felt that way.

Had sports-talk radio existed at that time, I would have been one of those guys I always bitch about when I listen to one of those stations. I'd have been "Charlie from Jersey." Back then, the way you talked about sports was just getting together with a bunch of guys and having an argument. You didn't call a radio show or a TV show. Those resources weren't available. You might end up with six guys sitting around, eating a pizza and arguing about sports. That was the way you did it.

Some of these guys were into different music. We had a lot of people who liked country or country rock. Jimmy Buffett had quite a few fans. There also were big followings for the Allman Brothers, Lynyrd Skynyrd, the Marshall Tucker Band, and Pure Prairie League. Then we had some guys who came into our section from Houston, and they were big fans of Willie Nelson and Jerry Jeff Walker.

I have always been a big Bruce Springsteen fan. The Boss was just getting cooking when I was in college in the mid-seventies. Obviously, I connected with the fact that he's from New Jersey, but I also liked him also because it seemed that almost every time I listened to one of his songs, there was something else with which I could identify, like "going down Highway 9" to the Jersey Shore. I liked the Beach Boys, too. They were from California, but they sang about the beach, and I was a guy who loved the beach on the Jersey Shore.

Believe it or not, one of my favorite activities at Notre Dame was going to church. I used to go to a folk mass at one of the girls' dorms, Breen-Phillips Hall, on Sunday night at eleven o'clock. It was the last mass on campus, and it would be packed, with at least three hundred people there. Song lyrics would be passed around, and everyone would sing.

The priest's homily would be directed to college kids. Not to older people or to younger people, but to us, college students. He'd always use a passage from the Bible that made sense in our everyday lives. He would find something that you had experienced sometime during your college career. Therefore, you felt connected with what he was talking about.

We had more than five hundred kids from New Jersey at Notre Dame, the third-highest total of any state. Being the entrepreneur that I was, I got together with a few other Jersey guys in my sophomore year to form a business—we called it the Notre Dame New Jersey Club—where we would haul the belongings of Notre Dame students from different parts of the state back and forth to campus at the beginning and end of each school year.

As a club, we were able to go to the registrar's office and get the names and addresses of all of the students from New Jersey to make them aware of the service. Then we rented three U-Haul trucks—one in north Jersey, one in central Jersey, and one in south Jersey—and charged for each item in a load. Our typical rates were twelve dollars for a trunk, ten dollars for a bicycle, and five dollars for boxes. I drove the central Jersey truck, which was parked at my house.

Once we got to school, we parked the trucks in a certain spot, and the students came and picked up their stuff. It was more expensive for us to rent the trucks going from the East Coast to the Midwest than in the other direction because of the greater demand for trucks in the East, but we made a profit—a significant profit. Everyone was happy to pay the money for the service—parents as well as students. For them it was a great convenience.

I was ambitious when it came to finding ways to make money. Through all four years of college, I spent summers working for the Town of Middlesex Parks Department. They hired about a dozen college kids to work on all of the parks and fields. We cut the grass, cleaned up the parks, and took care of the ball fields. It was a perfect summer job. It started at seven in the morning and went to three forty-five in the afternoon, Monday through Friday. After we went home and ate dinner, we came back to play ball on those same fields we'd worked on all day. We were a good grounds crew. We could get a field that was under six inches of water in the morning ready to play by five o'clock that night. I was an okay hitter, depending on what you were playing. It was easier to hit home runs in softball, which we played on smaller fields, than in baseball, which we basically played on football fields. It was 350 down the line, so there weren't too many balls going over the fence.

In high school, kids were separated into two social categories: "jocks" and "freaks." Those same categories carried over into college, but at Notre Dame, whether a kid looked like a jock or like a freak didn't make a difference, because everyone was involved in sports. Intramural sports are huge at Notre Dame. They provide a great diversion from studying. You're talking about a tough school academically, and a lot of people there spend a lot of time studying.

A great intramural event is the Bookstore Basketball Tournament, which is one of the most extraordinary things you'll see anywhere in a college setting. It's a single-elimination tournament for the whole campus—students, faculty, and other school employees participate—that starts out on all of the school's outdoor courts and ends up on the courts in front of the bookstore. The finals, usually held the last week of April, are played before thousands.

The tournament begins in early April with about six hundred teams. Varsity football players are invited to play in it, up to three per team. As Notre Dame's coach, I allow them to participate as long as they're in good academic standing and aren't injured. One member of the varsity basketball team also can be on each team, as long as that player is a senior and has used up his eligibility.

When football and basketball players are playing on their respective varsity teams, they obviously have a tremendous following from the other students. It's different for the ones who play in the Bookstore Basketball Tournament, because the other students love to remind them, through boos and catcalls, of the unfair athletic advantage they almost always have over the other competitors.

Another great Notre Dame tradition is interhall football. Every male dorm on campus has a team that plays in full pads and helmets. I played center for our dorm team, which was decent. In addition, my senior year, we won the finals in softball.

There is an intramural box-off, similar to a Golden Gloves tournament, called the Bengal Bouts. The event was founded by Dominic "Nappy" Napolitano in 1931 and got its name for raising funds for the Holy Cross Missions in Bangladesh. In 1923, Knute Rockne started the Notre Dame Boxing Club for the main purpose of keeping players in shape during the off-season, so a lot of the Bengal Bouts competitors have come from the football team. My junior year, the superheavyweight final was between a pair of outstanding Fighting Irish football players, tight end Ken McAfee and defensive end Ross Browner. McAfee hurt Browner early in the fight with what a lot of people thought was a cheap shot. Everyone started booing and the crowd got hostile, but Browner won.

One guy on my team, safety Tom Zbikowski, was a Golden Gloves boxer in Chicago with an amateur record of 75–15. In March 2006, the NCAA allowed him to turn professional (after

I signed off on it) while maintaining his eligibility for football as long as he doesn't take sponsorship money or endorsement money, or promote any boxing products.

No, Tom has never been invited to take part in the Bengal Bouts, and it's a safe bet that he never will.

3

An Assembly Line to Nowhere and a Classroom in a "Cave"

John Chironna was the first major influence on my coaching career.
(Courtesy of Morristown High School Yearbook Archive)

[John Chironna] didn't have to say anything, because the look said it all: "You don't know anything, so shut the hell up."

After I graduated from Notre Dame, I was offered one job in broadcasting at an NBC television affiliate by someone who had visited the campus to interview me. The pay was about six thousand dollars a year. I said, "I'm not doing that for that little money."

It was a big mistake. I should have taken something that would have gotten me into the field I wanted to pursue. Instead, I took some jobs in industry that I knew weren't going to lead to any careers and were jobs that I couldn't stand. That first year out of college was the one year that I really didn't know where my life was going. I was trying to find a niche, and it was a struggle.

I worked briefly at Ingersoll Rand in New Jersey. Then, with the help of a family friend, I got a job in labor relations at the Ford

Motor Company's Pinto plant, also in New Jersey. That was where I got my first bad taste of the mentality of people in a union. What I didn't like was the fact that the older these guys got, the more entitled they felt—as if they didn't have to do anything to earn the good money they were making. You had a lot of fifty-something guys, already on the job for thirty years, who had the union in their back pocket. No matter what they were told, they could tell you to go to hell.

I wasn't in the union. I was hired at a salary of about thirty-five thousand dollars a year, which was pretty good money back then—especially for a twenty-two-year-old. There also were some young guys on the assembly line. I knew that line, which was about a mile long, wasn't for me. Just imagine that your only job for an entire shift is putting tires on each car that rolls in front of you. Four lug nuts apiece. Front wheel, back wheel, front wheel, back wheel. On to the next car . . . and the one after that . . . and the one after that.

It was a depressing environment, but the thing that got to me the most was the union. Now, I have nothing against the United Auto Workers. I think it's great to have organizations that support the workers. My problem was with the people who had their thirty years in and, therefore, felt that they should be treated like royalty—especially by a young guy like me who would be viewed as a nobody.

At the same time, there were things that they bitched about that I agreed with, such as how often they were undermanned. I spent a lot of time actually going out on the line and picking up the slack. I did more of that than anything else. I was all over the place. One day there wouldn't be enough guys to put the tires on the cars, so I would go out there and do tires. Or there might be train cars to unload, so I would unload train cars. You know something? It felt good getting my hands dirty. It felt good going home after a long, hard day of physical labor.

There was a bar near the plant, and if you went in there after the day shift you'd see these guys, all in a row, getting drunk. The one time I did that I said to myself, Is this what I want to do? Do I want to be around this environment where you're depressed all day, and at the end of the day, after you've made a bunch of money, you go out and get drunk?

I already knew the answer. I quit after about six months.

ONE SUNDAY MORNING in 1979, I picked up the *Newark Star-Ledger*. Looking through the classifieds, I happened to see that two high schools in New Jersey, Boonton and Hillsboro, were looking for an English teacher–football coach. I hadn't been looking for the job, but I became intrigued.

While I was at Notre Dame, rather than just wasting my electives, I focused them so that I could be certified to teach English. I went through student teaching and everything else necessary to prepare me for an alternative in case things didn't work out in broadcasting.

At that point, I wondered where I was going with my life. Nothing was popping up in broadcasting. It was time to look at something else. Although I had done zero preparation for a job as a football coach, I still thought I had all of the answers. I thought, How tough could that be? Besides, as a teacher, I'd get summers off. It seemed like the perfect situation for me.

My father didn't quite see it that way, though. I remember him saying, "You went to Notre Dame to be a teacher?" I figured, I'm single. What do I have to lose? I interviewed at both schools in the same week and was offered both jobs. I chose Boonton, even though the teaching position would end up lasting only a year because I was replacing a woman who was on maternity leave.

In New Jersey, there are four levels of high school football, with Group One being the smallest schools and Group Four the largest. Boonton was a Group Two school at the time. John Stack, the varsity football coach at Boonton, wanted to do everything himself, so my duties as an assistant were very simple: do my job, as limited as it might be, and stay out of the way. He gave me a playbook, and I learned everything on my own. Stack was a very domineering guy. It didn't make much difference which assistants did what, because he was going to coach every position. Assistants were in charge of positions, but it was Stack's deal. It was his team, and nothing that any of us said or did would change that.

I thought I got along great with the kids in my classes. I thought that because I was younger, I was always perceived as one of the cooler teachers. There wasn't much of an age difference between us. Even when I had a problem with a kid in class, I would always handle it myself. I never threw a kid out of class. I would just humiliate him in front of his peers. Let's say a kid came into my class high, which was something you would deal with as a high school teacher. I'd say, "It's so good to see somebody who is really conscientious and realizes that you need to pass English to graduate from high school. Now here's a prime example. . . ."

Then I'd go into more of my sarcastic rhetoric. After I got done humiliating him, he'd be ready to crawl underneath a chair. It was effective. We'd never have a problem again.

The kids would not come late to my class. The other teachers got angry with kids running in the hallway all of the time to be in their seats in my classroom before the bell rang. The kids also brought their homework to class on time.

My approach didn't sit too well with everybody. The people in administration were used to having everyone else just send their problem kids down to the office. I never sent anyone down to the office. What good was it going to do to have a kid go down to the office and then get thrown out of school for three days? I would rather try and fix it myself, try and keep the kid in school, before I would turn it over to somebody else.

I had five classes at Boonton. I taught juniors and seniors, but mainly seniors. I had some football players in class. I treated them the same as everyone else, and they didn't act any differently because I was their teacher. They just knew me better than some of the other kids did. They knew my personality. They knew what was coming when someone got out of line. They'd start laughing before it started, as long as it was directed at someone other than them.

I didn't know or learn much about coaching football. It wasn't like I was being groomed to be a coach at that time. It was more like being a camp counselor than a coach. In practice it was, "You've got those guys . . . you've got those guys . . . you've got those guys . . . but that's the boss, and he's running everything." Stack would give us a set of drills that he wanted us to take the players through, and that was what we did. I don't even remember what position group I had.

Stack was constantly cursing out players. It was negative reinforcement all of the time, and that didn't fire me up. It didn't fire up the players, either. We went 0–9 that season. I wasn't demoralized, though, because I liked being part of a team. I liked the camaraderie. At that time, I didn't care about the won-loss record. For a guy who loves sports, it doesn't get any better than being a part of the competition, win or lose. For the first time in a long time, I felt I was a part of it.

I got involved in other sports, too. I coached the eighth-grade basketball team. I was going to be the freshman baseball coach, but there weren't enough guys, so the school had just a varsity team and a jayvee team, and I went up and helped the varsity baseball coach for the year.

My introduction to coaching, as Stack approached it, was a rude awakening. I thought, If this is what coaching is all about, I don't know if I want to do this for very long.

At the end of the season, there was an awards banquet for the high school football coaches in Morris County. Every coaching staff in the county attended. Being the young pup on the Boonton staff, I was the sacrificial lamb that had to ride with Coach Stack—who was driving—to the banquet, which was way out at a country club in Netcong. After the event, he was hanging with a lot of the old-time coaches. Some of the younger assistants were leaving, so I caught a ride back with them.

On his way home, Coach Stack got in a car accident. He ended up paralyzed from the waist down.

After I heard that, I had to sit down and say, Well, how lucky am I? Whether I too would have been injured, or even killed, I will never know. All I do know is that I wasn't in that car. I felt very fortunate that nothing happened to me. (Coach Stack would be able to continue coaching football at Boonton from a wheelchair before leaving to coach at another school in Florida.)

I sat there that night and wondered, Why wasn't I in that car?

The answer that kept coming back to me was, This is what I'm supposed to do. I'm supposed to teach and coach.

AT THE END of the year, the administrators at Boonton brought me in and told me that the teacher I had replaced was coming back from maternity leave, so I was let go. One of the things I find humorous now is that I'm on the Boonton High School Wall of Fame. They have different bricks for people who have come out of Boonton and become successful. I was there one year, and my name is engraved on a brick on their Wall of Fame: "Charlie Weis, Head Coach, University of Notre Dame." The principal even wrote me a letter that said if I was ever in the area, I should stop in, and he would be glad to show me the Wall of Fame.

I wasn't out of work for long. Morristown, which is a Group Four school with an excellent reputation, was looking for an English teacher–football coach. Morristown is more of a cultural smorgasbord than Boonton. The students there ranged from the poorest of the poor to the rich, and included every race, creed, and color. I interviewed for the job and got it right away. This was not an opening created by a maternity leave. This was a job that I could stay in for longer than a year. I didn't want another situation where I get close to the kids, liked what I was doing, became part of the town—and then, all of a sudden, was gone.

The environment in the football program was totally different from what it was at Boonton because of the way the head coach, John Chironna, ran the whole operation. First of all, although he was clearly the boss, and a strict disciplinarian and brilliant guy, Coach Chironna actually let his assistant coaches do their jobs. He had an offensive coordinator and a defensive coordinator. He had an offensive line coach and a defensive line coach. He had a linebackers coach, a running backs coach, and a defensive backs coach. And he had a receivers coach—me.

I was on the very bottom rung of the ladder. I was a grunt.

In the summertime, before we started teaching, we were already involved in football. Summer workouts were all organized, from the weight room on up. Practice was organized. Everything Morristown did was as different from Boonton as day was from night. It was what I had envisioned coaching football was going to be. I thought, My God! This is what the big time is.

We covered details like teaching receivers how to "block run force," which is a matter of knowing whether or not to block the cornerback or the safety involved in stopping the run, and then learning how to do it. We also covered the explanation of the "passing tree," which consists of numbers, zero through nine, that tell you whether a guy is running a short, intermediate, or deep route, in or out. To call pass plays, a lot of teams in the NFL use numbers that indicate the routes that everyone's running. For instance, "909" could be two "go" routes, and the tight end stays in to block. When people talk about a "nine" route in the NFL, they're talking about a straight, deep go route. When they talk about a "seven" route, they're talking about a corner route—to the corner of the end zone. When they talk about "fives" and "sixes," they're talking about in cuts and out cuts. When they talk about "three" and "four," one's a slant route and the other's a diagonal route. I don't remember learning about any of those things at Boonton.

My knowledge of the game still was minimal. Like most armchair quarterbacks, I watched the games and bitched about the play calling, but I didn't actually understand the game. I started to learn it from John, who was also the athletic director. He had an old, dark, asbestos-ridden little office in the basement of the school that was nicknamed "the Cave." It contained a desk, some beat-up couches, a projector, a movie screen, and an old chalkboard where you would always see him doodling with Xs and Os, lines and arrows.

John was always puffing on either a cigar or a pipe. He had graying hair that he always wore pushed back. He looked and acted like a professor. John had played football at Bucknell with the late George Young, who was the general manager of the New York Giants when I was at Morristown. They were best buddies and would have philosophical arguments all of the time. In the early 1960s, John had been the head football coach at the University of Rhode Island.

He was tough. He was an in-your-face kind of guy, although he didn't swear as much as Stack did. Of all of the head coaches I've been around, he had the cleanest mouth, but that doesn't mean he was a saint.

He was very well respected. Not loved by everyone, because he wasn't trying to be everyone's friend, but respected. I liked the way he took a multicultural group of students and meshed them together. You had blacks, whites, and Hispanics, but you'd never know the difference, because they just saw themselves as being part of a team.

I spent as much time around Chironna as possible, picking up all of the football knowledge I could from him, which was a lot. Because I was also teaching English, my visits to the Cave were either early in the morning or late at night. The other assistant coaches on the staff were around too, and a lot of them were around a lot of hours. When the other assistants were in the room, John was usually setting up the offensive and defensive game plans. As the youngest member of the staff, still learning about the game, I would sit quietly most of the time during those sessions and just listen. That was when I would learn what we were doing. When it was just the two of us, John would teach me why we were doing what we were doing.

For instance, if you were blocking run force and were going to run outside, he would say, "Three-four on the corner." That meant that the wide receiver was going to come in and crack the safety, and the tight end was going to go out and block the corner to create a natural running lane. He explained that rather than trying to stretch the defense horizontally, we'd create our own running lane.

A lot of teams like to stretch the defense by running the ball with their line moving to one side or the other, while the back looks for whatever lane he can find as he tries to get to the corner. That's called "zone blocking." That's what the Indianapolis Colts liked to do with Edgerrin James. You'd often see him trying to get to the corner, where he would then turn upfield. If he didn't have the corner, somewhere along the line he still had to turn it upfield. Edgerrin ran those plays as well as anyone in the NFL, not only because of his physical talent, but also because of his instincts— his ability to know when to make that turn.

What we were doing at Morristown was called "gap blocking." John wanted to create a running lane because he wanted the back to know where he was supposed to go and then just have to react if it didn't work out that way. We didn't use zone blocking, because there were very few backs, especially at the high school level, who could decide like Edgerrin when to make that cut.

The biggest lesson I learned that year was that I didn't know anything. Many times Chironna would say something, and I'd think, How could I be so stupid? Why couldn't I figure that out on my own? Why did somebody have to tell that to me? Why couldn't I just come up with it?

Sure, he often had to put me in my place because I still thought I had all of the answers. He had a simple way of letting you know that you knew nothing. All Chironna had to do was give you a look. He didn't have to say anything, because the look said it all: "You don't know anything, so shut the hell up."

Listening to Chironna, the game of football started to make more and more sense to me. When he was talking to the players, I'd be looking at a play and wondering, How are they ever going to learn how to do this? Then he'd stand up there and talk to the team. He'd describe the same play that had seemed so complicated when I looked at it on my own, and I'd say, "I can't believe it's that easy."

John always felt that game day was for the players, and that a football coach's main job took place from the beginning of the week to the end of the week. Did coaches have an involvement on game day? Yes. Coaches in football, more than in many other sports, have a lot to do with the outcome of a game. John saw game day as a culmination of all of the work that we put in, but that ultimately it was for the players. If they didn't know what to do by that point, then we had no chance.

Another lesson John taught me was that to be successful in coaching, you have to put everything into it. You can't just be a game-day coach. There are a lot of guys at every level that like everyone to see them on game day, but don't want to put in the blood, sweat, and tears to be successful. There are guys like that even in the NFL. They're the last ones to get to the office and the first ones to leave.

John was the first to tell me that coaching football was a year-round job. As athletic director he had to support the other sports, but what was really important to him was teaching and coaching football. That was his passion.

I was enlightened by John's cerebral approach to the game. For the first time in my life I was truly intrigued with an occupation. I finally found something that made me say, Hey, I like this. I could see myself doing this. It was different from the feeling I'd had at Boonton. There, I felt that fate was telling me that I should do it, but now I was actually saying, Okay. Now we've got something here.

AT MORRISTOWN, I taught all juniors and seniors in the general English classes, as opposed to the college-prep kids. None of the other teachers wanted the general English classes because it was a rougher crowd, but I loved those kids. This was back when the television series *Welcome Back, Kotter* was still on the air. Gabe Kotter had his "Sweathogs." For us it was "Weis's Dirtbags" because I used to call everyone in those classes "dirtbags." The kids actually had T-shirts made up that said "Weis's Dirtbags."

The first two years I was at Morristown, I was the jayvee basketball coach. John made me take the job because he had no one else to do it. One day he just told me, "You're the jayvee basketball coach." I had no say in the matter. I didn't know much about coaching basketball, and he knew that, but he told me that he liked my enthusiasm.

Our jayvee basketball team actually ended up being good, winning most of our games, but it was not because I was a good basketball coach. We had good players, and I just didn't screw it up.

We were more athletic than most teams. We just ran up and down the court and pressed the whole game.

That first experience as the coach in charge had its ups and downs. I was the boss, which was fun, but I didn't have a passion for basketball. I had followed the Knicks, but my interest had been from a broadcaster's perspective. It was just like the way I felt about the Rangers. I loved watching them, but I didn't skate, so I knew my involvement would never go any further than being a spectator.

After those first two years, the varsity basketball coach resigned. A guy from Morristown named Muzz Lindsey, who was the head basketball coach at Bailey-Ellard, a Catholic high school in Madison, was John's choice to fill the position. Suddenly, one of the teachers in the district applied for the job. Being a member of the union, he filed a grievance saying that Muzz was not a teacher in the district, and because this teacher was, he should get the job. I don't think the teacher actually wanted the job, but the grievance was his way of letting Chironna know that he wasn't going to be able to just handpick anyone he wanted. The teacher won the grievance.

Shortly thereafter, Chironna told me, "You're the head varsity basketball coach."

I'd gone from never having been a basketball coach, to coaching two years of jayvee, to becoming the head coach of the varsity basketball team at a Group Four school. John's rationale was that the decision had less to do with just shafting that other teacher (although that was definitely a part of it) than with the chance to give me some head-coaching experience.

This was a tough job. First of all, there were a lot of kids on the team who weren't all that disciplined; these were a bunch of renegades. Plus, after a very good season the previous year, this was going to be a down year for the basketball program. We had lost three big, fast, athletic players—a six-nine center and a couple of guys who were six-five—to graduation. All my little guys from the jayvee were the ones who would be playing on varsity.

John thought it would be a good idea for me to get a taste of what it was like to be in charge of a team going through a rough season. He wanted me to get hardened.

We struggled for a while. I threw two starters off the team for disciplinary reasons. Then two other kids quit after I sat them down for missing practice on game day. I had a rule that if you missed school or practice the day before or the day of a game, you weren't going to play in the game. I wanted the kids to be account-able in school as well as on the team. I didn't want a kid blowing off school and then showing up to play in a game. I also didn't want them to think that if they missed practice, I still owed it to them to let them play in the game.

The rule was important enough for me to include as part of a code-of-conduct contract that I had each player sign, along with his parent or guardian, before the season. That night, the father of the two kids who had missed practice that day came up to me after the game and said, "Why didn't you play my kids?"

"They signed a contract," I said. "So did you."

Case closed.

I followed a lot of the previous coach's practice regimen. Also, my jayvee basketball coach was a pretty smart basketball guy, so I implemented a lot of the schemes that he suggested. He had played basketball at a small college, and he knew Bobby Knight's motion offense and John Wooden's 2-2-1 full-court press. It was copycat stuff, but it was enough to help us, and I wasn't afraid to lean on him.

My greatest challenge had nothing to do with basketball, though. It was dealing with the group of kids on the team. The basketball program did not have the same level of discipline that the football program had. What I was trying to do was make the basketball program's discipline parallel the football program's.

It was like pulling teeth, but it worked. At one point, we were 4–7. We had to get to .500 just to make the county tournament, and we got there. We were the tenth seed. We played the first seed in the semifinals and kicked the crap out of them. We played the second seed in the finals and kicked the crap out of them, too.

That was rewarding. I felt validated because I'd stuck to my guns, discipline-wise, and we still ended up winning a championship.

4

Nothing to Lose . . .
and a Career to Gain

Joe Morrison gave me a huge break when he brought me to
South Carolina. *(Courtesy of South Carolina Athletics Media Relations)*

"If you want to be a [graduate assistant] for us, come on down."

—Joe Morrison,
former South Carolina football coach

During the '84–'85 school year, all I wanted to be was a head football coach in high school. John Chironna planned to retire soon, but I didn't know if I would get the opportunity at Morristown. Three people from the staff were likely replacements for Chironna: George Bellias, longtime defensive coordinator Jim Bassano, and me. George wound up getting the job.

Still, coaching high school football was what life was all about for me at that point . . . or so I thought. My perspective changed on one miserable, cold, rainy November day in 1984. It happened almost the instant that I walked into the smoke-filled teachers' lounge at Morristown. This was back when people were allowed to smoke pretty much wherever they wanted. As a nonsmoker, I didn't like that very much.

The worst part, though, was the attitude of the people in that room. All I heard was everyone bitching, saying things like, "Just twelve more years until I retire." I was saying to myself, Twelve more years until I retire? What an awful attitude. I can't do this. This is not for me. It reminded me of the Pinto plant, and I'd hated that place.

Joe Morrison, the University of South Carolina football coach and former great running back and receiver for the Giants, came up to Morristown to recruit a defensive back–running back for us named Kenny Salley. As a kid, I had watched Morrison play for the Giants from my seat in the bleachers at Yankee Stadium, and on television. When TV coverage of the Giants' home games was blacked out, as was the case back then, I listened to him play on the radio.

I had a chance to speak with Morrison while he was at our school, and I asked him how you got to be a college coach. He talked about starting out as a graduate assistant. Then he said, "If you want to be a GA for us, come on down."

There was nothing keeping me from heading down to Columbia, South Carolina, in 1985. I was twenty-nine years old. My father had died of a heart attack in 1983. I knew that my mother, who had been taking care of him for five years after he had suffered an earlier heart attack and stroke, would be fine on her own. She was within a couple of years of fulfilling her dream of seeing all five of her children graduate from college in four years. She had seen my older sister, Karen, graduate from the University of Pennsylvania with a degree in physical therapy; my brother Michael graduate from Upsala College in Newark, New Jersey, with a degree in accounting; and my brother Peter graduate from West Point with a degree in engineering. I'll never forget my mother saying to me, after my youngest brother, Pat, graduated from the University of Tennessee with a degree in electrical engineering, "If I die tomorrow, I'll feel like my life is complete because all of my kids graduated from college."

I took Coach Morrison up on his offer. I gave up about forty thousand dollars a year for teaching and coaching multiple sports at Morristown to go to South Carolina, where I'd be a graduate assistant for nothing. All I got was tuition, room, board, books, and fees, but I was single, so I didn't view it as a gamble. What do you have to lose? I asked myself. If you don't like doing that, you go do something else. I could always go teach again because there weren't many male English teachers who could coach sports.

All I knew about the University of South Carolina was that its football program had been good in '84. As a matter of fact, the Gamecocks actually had a chance to play for the national championship. They had a 9–0 record and were ranked as high as No. 2 in the country before losing to Navy. They ended up 10–2, losing to Oklahoma State in the Gator Bowl.

People called Coach Morrison "the Man in Black" because he used to wear black all the time. He was a very intimidating guy. He didn't talk a lot. He didn't feel he had to. He was just a good old country guy from Lima, Ohio.

There were no limits then on how many graduate assistants and student assistants a college could have. It wasn't like today, when the NCAA limits each school to two graduate assistants and nine assistant coaches. There were about ten graduate assistants and student assistants—most of them guys on the team whose eligibility was up—on the South Carolina coaching staff. I was one of the older GAs. I wasn't someone who had just graduated college, so I felt I was going to be able to outwork everyone to rise up.

Plus, I had been coaching in high school, so I felt I had a clue about how to coach. I believed that the combination of coaching in high school and my work ethic would give me the opportunity to move past a lot of the other GAs.

Although I worked for the defensive backs coach, Tom Mc-Mahon, Coach Morrison also gave me a bunch of personal stuff to do for him. He might ask me to drop off paperwork at a law office or some sort of errand like that, or to follow a player around on campus to make sure that the kid was going to class. I remember doing that with a freshman. I made sure that he would see me following him through his entire schedule every day, so that he knew it wasn't going to be just a one-day deal. I didn't like babysitting, but I understood why I was doing it.

I never felt Coach Morrison was picking on me. He was never demeaning or condescending. I thought that he was picking me out because he had confidence in me. As he started to trust me more and more, he gave me more and more to do.

The two men who did the most to help further my football knowledge at that time were McMahon and the defensive coordinator, Tom Gadd. Whenever McMahon was coaching the defensive backs, I'd be with him just absorbing what he was teaching them. He was a good teacher. Coach Gadd was good at not making you feel like you were a nonentity. I didn't say much, but he had no problem letting me go into a defensive staff meeting and take in everything the coaches were saying and doing. With Chironna I was looking at both sides of the ball. Now I was worried about just the defense.

The lack of an income did put enough of a strain on my finances that I decided to leave the university at one point for a job in Columbia, South Carolina, with one of Coach Morrison's friends in commercial real estate. After one day of that, I was ready to quit. There was a going-away party for me on Friday at the school, I went to work on Saturday, and on Sunday I came back to the school asking, "Is my job still available?" Fortunately it was. The experience just reinforced that coaching football was something I wanted to play out, and however long it took, I wanted to see if I could do it.

A year later, Coach Morrison hired one of his best friends, Joe Lee Dunn, to be his new defensive coordinator in place of Gadd, who left for Utah to become defensive coordinator under Jim Fassel. Dunn made me a volunteer assistant, working with outside linebackers and defensive ends. Even though I was a "volunteer," under NCAA rules I could be paid, so now I was getting some money for my efforts. The job was easy because Joe Lee wouldn't listen to anybody. He would break down all of the videotape himself, then walk into a meeting of the defensive coaching staff and say, "Here's the game plan. This is what we're doing."

Veteran coaches didn't like that, because they wanted to be able to give their ideas. For a young guy, it was perfect, because all I had to do was have him tell me what we were doing and then teach it to the players. I was not looking to give him ideas. I just had to make sure the guys we had knew what they were doing.

Joe Lee liked to blitz a lot. In his scheme, you had inside linebackers both rushing the passer and playing coverage, and you had outside linebackers and defensive ends doing the same. It's sort of what teams do today with outside linebackers in the 3–4 defense. I was intrigued with learning what to do myself and then making sure I could stay one step ahead of the players, who performed pretty well.

In 1988, my fourth season at South Carolina, I was made assistant recruiting coordinator. The fancy title didn't mean much.

It was just a way for Coach Morrison to increase my salary. After that '88 season he went a step further by offering to make me a full-fledged outside linebackers coach while also extending my contract.

On Sunday, February 5, 1989, I had lunch with Coach Morrison and the athletic director to finalize the deal that would pay me for the rest of that year as well as the following year. After that, I left on a recruiting trip to Richmond, Virginia. Later that day, Coach Morrison went to play racquetball. Afterward, he said he wasn't feeling well. The trainer checked him and said that as a precaution, he should go to the hospital. Coach Morrison agreed, but didn't want to make a big deal about it by having an ambulance show up with sirens and flashing lights. He planned to go after taking a shower.

About three o'clock that afternoon, he dropped dead of a heart attack in the shower.

I didn't find out about it until I got back from Richmond at around six o'clock that evening. A friend of mine called and said, "Sorry about Coach Morrison."

"What about Coach Morrison?" I said.

"He died."

Of course, I was stunned. An hour or so later, the staff had a meeting with the athletic director. Joe Lee Dunn became the interim head coach because we were three days from signing day—when recruits commit to which colleges they will attend—and someone had to be in charge at least temporarily. We knew that once a permanent replacement was hired, the assistant coaches would be fired because the new guy would want to bring in his own people.

Sure enough, Sparky Woods, from Appalachian State, got the

permanent head-coaching position, and the rest of us were let go, with the exception of one assistant coach who had recently been hired. I stuck around until May of '89, to help with spring recruiting, then left.

I WAS STILL in South Carolina, going through the transition from one coaching staff to the next, when Bill Parcells, who was coaching the Giants, hired Al Groh, who had been the offensive coordinator at South Carolina in my last year there, to be his linebackers coach. Bill Belichick, who had been coaching the linebackers while also serving as defensive coordinator, became the defensive coordinator–secondary coach. One day Tim Rooney, who was the Giants' director of pro personnel, mentioned to Al that he was looking for some guys who would help break down videotape of the younger players in the league, to give him more time to work on other things. Tim's duties included evaluating all of the guys in the league in case one of them became available or the Giants wanted to go after a guy in a trade. Every team in the league does that.

"I know a guy who's got a lot of time on his hands," Al said, referring to me.

Tim then sent me a bunch of tapes with the names and numbers of the players to watch, some blank forms for my grades and comments, and just turned me loose. The grades were based on a numbering system, with nine being the highest a player could get. If you had someone in the sevens, that was a can't-miss superstar.

A couple days later, I sent the tapes back to him, along with my grades on each player. Tim was surprised I had sent them back that quickly, but that wasn't all that surprised him. There was a linebacker for the Philadelphia Eagles who I thought stunk, and I said as much in my report. It turned out that Tim agreed with exactly what I said. I think he thought that I would be enamored with the player's name—which I honestly don't remember—but I wasn't. I just gave my objective opinion. I found out later that Tim told Parcells, "This guy's a little different here."

Tim sent me more tapes to grade. I would write them up and send them back to him as quickly as the first batch.

In the meantime, I interviewed for a head football coaching job at Franklin High School in New Jersey. I got the job and moved back to New Jersey in May. I wasn't going to get involved with that job until the summertime, when I would begin running the off-season program—weight lifting and so forth—so I went up to Giants Stadium every day and did more tapes.

Everyone in the building knew who I was. Every once in a while Parcells would say hello to me and maybe follow it up with, "Tell me a little bit about yourself." Or I'd say, "Hey, Coach, how's it going?" It was never any buddy-buddy stuff.

I continued breaking down tapes even after the Giants began training camp that summer at Farleigh Dickinson University in Madison, New Jersey. I would get there early in the morning and stay there as late as I could. Even when we started workouts in the evening at Franklin, I would go to the Giants' camp at the crack of dawn and stay until about three o'clock in the afternoon.

When training camp came around, the Giants' scouts started writing reports on all of the guys in camp. I did that, too. Tim had me watch the defensive linemen during practice. I followed them through every drill, took notes, and the next day studied the tape of the practice. Tim would also let me sit in on the scouts' meetings. Every once in a while I'd be asked a question, and I'd give my two cents.

I remember one meeting, about the defensive linemen in camp, when I was just sitting and listening to the discussion about a particular member of that group. Finally one of the scouts asked for my opinion.

"I don't think he's worth a crap," I said.

I just gave the answer in my Jersey vernacular. Everyone started laughing—everyone but Lamar Leachman, the defensive line coach. It turned out that the player was a guy he liked. He wasn't too happy with me.

The opinions I formed and the reports I wrote were based on what I saw, not on what I heard. I think that's why I hit it off with Tim. He liked the fact that I was objective despite being surrounded by people whose views and reputations could easily have tainted my thoughts. That was something I learned from Tim. To this day I tell my players and coaches, "I go only by what I see. I don't go by what anybody says to me."

FRANKLIN, A GROUP three school, had a good football team, having lost in the state finals the year before. The previous head coach had left to take another coaching job in north Jersey. He had been very popular with the players. He was also African American, and there were a lot of African Americans on the team.

Our views on how to do things weren't the same. I was more of a stickler on academics. Not that he didn't care about academics— he did—but I was just more of a stickler. As a matter of fact, at the end of each day, before football practice, every sophomore, junior, and senior on the team would go to an hour-long study hall that I ran. Study hall would last from 2:30 P.M. to 3:30 P.M., and then we'd go on the field at 4:00 and practice until 6:00.

When I got there a lot of kids were struggling academically, and I felt the study hall provided a venue where I knew they were going to do at least an hour of homework a day because I was running it. I also would let kids use that hour to get extra help from the teacher of a subject in which they were struggling the most, but only if that teacher signed them out and signed them back in. I didn't run study hall just to keep players academically eligible for football, I ran it because it was the right thing to do. I did it to emphasize how important I thought academics were.

I wish I could say the same about how the people in the administration at Franklin handled my hiring. When I interviewed, they told me I was going to teach two classes a day of remedial English, first and second period. They also told me that they had two openings, one in physical education and one in guidance, and if I had any assistant coaches I wanted to recommend who were also certified as either PE teachers or guidance counselors, then they could be hired to fill those spots.

I lined up two guys who were ready to be part of my coaching staff. Then, after I took the job and just before the start of the school year, those positions were suddenly no longer available. They had been "RIF'd," which is an acronym for a reduction in force. On top of that, I no longer had two classes a day of remedial English. The administrators ended up giving me a full schedule of five classes of regular English a day.

As a result, I decided that as soon as the season was over, I was resigning, regardless of how we did. We had made a deal, and they had broken it. The only reason I didn't resign immediately was that I felt I had put in too much of an investment to bow out on those kids at that time.

Just as I had done when I became varsity basketball coach at Morristown, I drew up a code-of-conduct contract that I made the players and their parents or guardians sign before we started playing. Things like missing class or getting into any sort of trouble would be subject to disciplinary action. Everyone signed it, and everyone understood what the rules were. This way, if there was a violation, I didn't have to deal with what the penalty was going to be, because it was clearly stated in the contract.

My offensive captain, who was a running back and middle linebacker, missed a class on the day of the first game of the season. I didn't play him, and that almost resulted in a mutiny. Then we won the game, 68–6, so the residual effect of the episode was that players saw we could win with or without any single player; the guys also started to understand, Hey, he's not messing around.

We won the state championship that year, easily beating Ocean Township. The major lesson I learned from that experience was that you don't have to circumvent your own convictions to win. You can make the players go to class, make them follow a code of conduct, and still win. That's exactly what I'm doing now.

The Monday after we won the state title I walked into the office of the athletic director and told him, "I'm resigning."

Then I walked into the office of the principal and said, "I'm resigning."

There was a new superintendent who asked me to go over and talk with him. I did. I told him, "I'm resigning."

To get me to reconsider, the superintendent offered to honor my original deal. Isn't it amazing how everything suddenly changes after you win a state championship?

"No, we had a deal before that was broken," I said. "I'm still resigning."

I ended up teaching through Christmas, and that was it.

5

Sometimes Your Prayers Are Answered and Your Buttons Are Pushed

My prayers were answered when the Giants hired me.

(Courtesy of the New York Giants)

> "You've been in the league for five minutes. . . .
> So why don't you just sit there and keep your
> mouth shut!"

> —Bill Parcells

In January 1990, I accepted a job offer in South Carolina, thanks to a connection I'd had while coaching down there, to sell long-distance telephone service to businesses for ten cents a minute—not a bad deal at that time. I had an office and a secretary and a solid base of customers. It was a good situation.

Less than a month into the job came an opportunity to truly get my foot in the coaching door of the NFL. After Lamar Leachman left the Giants to coach the defensive line for the Lions, Bill Parcells decided he was going to move Romeo Crennel from special-teams coach to defensive line coach. He also promoted Mike Sweatman from the assistant special-teams coach and defensive quality-control coach to special-teams coach. Now Bill was looking to hire an assistant special-teams coach and defensive quality-control coach. From what I would later find out, he told Tim Rooney he was looking for a smart young guy who was single, energetic, and would work endless hours. In other words, someone who had no life.

"Well, you had a guy just like that in here last summer breaking down tape," Tim said, referring to me. "You really should talk with him."

One day I got a phone call. My secretary said, "Bill Parcells is on the phone." I figured it was just one of my friends busting my chops.

"Yeah, sure," I said. "Go ahead and put him through."

I picked up the phone and, treating the call like the joke I was sure it was, I said, "Hey, Bill, how's it going?"

The second I heard his voice I knew it was really him. Then I went from, "Hey, Bill," to, "Hey, Coach."

He flew me up for an interview, which lasted all day. He must have spent an hour of it on a StairMaster. I wasn't in awe of him. I was just looking to get the job with the team I had loved my whole life. I wanted to work for Coach Parcells. I wanted to work for one of the greatest owners in the league, Wellington Mara. I mean, it was the Giants.

Later, Bill had me talk with Sweatman because I was going to be taking his old job, and Bill wanted him to point me in the right direction. Bill also gave me some game tape of another team's offense to break down. Breaking down tape of an opponent's offense is the main duty of a defensive quality-control coach (the offensive quality-control coach does the same with the opposing defense). You have a form on which you draw up the whole offense, including the formation, down, and distance, where the ball is located, and what every guy is doing on every play. You draw up the defense, too, so that the defensive coaches can see how that offense attacks somebody else's defense. I had a little crash course on how to do it, but when you're first learning, it takes forever to do. It took me forever.

After I finally finished, Bill said, "I'll let you know," and sent me on my way.

I was one of several guys that he interviewed, so I knew it would be competitive. A week went by, and I didn't hear anything. Another week, and still no word. Then a third week passed, and, again, nothing.

At first I was a nervous wreck, but the longer it went without anyone being hired, the better I felt my chances were. If he'd intended to hire a guy that he knew or who had an inside track on the job, I figured he'd have done it right away. The longer it went meant that I was still in the picture.

I also prayed a lot. I told God that if I got the job I would never ask for anything else, personally, for as long as I lived. I might ask for something for a family member or a close friend, but not for me. If I got the job, that would be it.

A month after the interview, after returning home on a Sunday from my brother Peter's wedding in Oklahoma, I found a message waiting for me. It was from Bill Parcells. I called him right away, and he offered me the job. I never asked him how much it paid; it didn't matter. On Monday morning I resigned from my sales job, packed whatever I could in my car, and headed north. I was sitting in the parking lot of Giants Stadium on Tuesday morning.

Bill ended up paying me seventy-five thousand dollars, which was a lot more than I was expecting to get. Even today there are a lot of guys doing quality control that start off at only twenty-five thousand dollars. He paid me above and beyond my worth. I doubt that Bill thought I was worth that much either. I think he was just trying to do me right.

In breaking down tapes of opposing offenses, I had to stay one week ahead of the schedule so that the defensive coaches would have my work by the Saturday morning a week before a Sunday game. That was the time they would begin preparing for the next opponent. On Monday, they were going to put together a scouting report for the defense, and that was going to be based on the games that I broke down.

In the beginning, I was awful. It would take me ten hours to do one game tape (eventually, I would get that down to three hours). The forms I turned in had all kinds of mistakes. Most of all, they lacked detail. For instance, I might see a formation with three wide receivers on one play, and then, if I saw another play with the same formation, I might write down that there were three wide receivers out there when, in fact, the third wide receiver was actually a running back. If you get that wrong, then you're not going to be able to properly explain why the defense treated the formation differently from when there actually were three wide receivers on the field.

The defensive coaches would give me specific stuff to break down, but they didn't have time to teach me how to do it. They would just point out my mistakes, and then it was up to me to learn from them. As the defensive coordinator, Belichick would go over my reports and say, "Here's what's wrong here . . . here's what's wrong here . . . here's what's wrong here. . . ."

Sometimes, one of the other defensive coaches—Groh or Crennel—would give me projects where I was to look for a certain weakness that a team might have that could be exploited. For instance, they might say, "Check the stances of the offensive linemen." Every once in a blue moon I'd come up with something. I remember watching a left guard for the Cardinals who was giving away a lot more than I'm sure he and his coaches wanted him to be giving away. When it was a pass, he had one stance. When it was a run to the right, he had another stance. When it was a run to the left, he had a different stance.

So when the Cardinals' offense would go to the line of scrimmage, our inside linebackers would look at him and be able to tell everyone else on defense what play was coming. Finding those keys was usually what the defensive coaches did. When you told them you had something, they always made a point to confirm its accuracy because they weren't going to give anything to the players unless it was a guarantee. In the case of that Cardinal lineman, it was one hundred percent.

Besides breaking down tapes, I was also helping Sweatman coach special teams. In a typical week during the season, I would be in meetings with our defensive coaching staff until nine o'clock at night. Then I'd go meet with Sweatman until eleven o'clock. At eleven, I'd start to break down tape. For a lot of guys in quality control, breaking down tape is all they ever do. However, if you want to learn what the team is going to be doing on defense and special teams in the game that week, you have to sit in on those meetings in addition to doing your quality-control duties.

It made for a long, hard day. It was a true grinder's job. There were a lot of nights when I got only a couple of hours of sleep, but what kept me going was that I saw myself learning football. I was forced to learn because I was doing it by myself. I was learning what offenses and defenses did, because I was watching tape after tape after tape.

Eventually I started picking things up faster. I'd see the same formation late in a game that I'd seen earlier and know what was happening before the play was even run. I could start predicting what was going to happen based on what I was seeing. An example would be the Washington Redskins. Every time it got to be first-and-ten, Joe Gibbs would like to throw the ball twenty yards down the field on a play-action pass. I knew what was going to happen when a team lined up with the receivers grouped to one side in a "bunch" formation, or when the backs were offset a particular way, or when the halfback cheated in a certain direction, or when the wide receivers took a tighter split.

ONE OF MY biggest eye-opening experiences came that summer in training camp. We were in a staff meeting and Parcells asked Sweatman, "If something happens to [Dave] Meggett, who's our backup punt returner?"

Sweatman hemmed and hawed a bit. He didn't have an answer ready. Because he always had me standing back with the punt returners in practice, I chimed right in: "[Mark] Ingram would be next, Coach, then [Stephen] Baker."

I figured that I had done the right thing by helping Sweatman out. I figured wrong. Parcells looked at me and said, "You've been in the league for five minutes. No one gives a shit about what you think. So why don't you just sit there and keep your mouth shut!"

That was basically what I did through every staff meeting I attended from that day forward . . . until we were playing Detroit about midway through the season. The Lions were using a run-and-shoot offense, something that almost no other team was doing at the time, and had scored twenty or more points in eight of their previous nine games. They were also undefeated.

During our Wednesday practice, Jeff Hostetler threw for about a thousand yards and ten touchdown passes against our starting defense as the show-team quarterback running the run-and-shoot.

In the staff meeting that night, Parcells looked at Belichick and Groh and said, "Okay, you wizards"—that was one of many sarcastic terms Bill used to refer to his assistant coaches—"that might have been the worst football practice I've ever seen in my life. You guys had better go fix it!"

After that we went into a defensive staff meeting. I'd not said another word in a meeting since the comment that had drawn Parcells's wrath earlier in the season, and I had no intention of speaking up again, even though I was familiar with the run-and-shoot because that was what we ran at South Carolina. I just sat there and I listened to the coaches talking about what they could do against the Lions' explosive offense.

Then Belichick turned to me and said, "Got any suggestions?"

As smart as Belichick was, he was never afraid to ask for advice, regardless of who you were. Even if he disagreed with you, he would always listen. That's one of the reasons why he is so successful today.

"Well, Coach," I said, "I can just tell you what Texas A&M did to stop the University of Houston."

At the time, John Jenkins was running the run-and-shoot at the University of Houston, and that Cougars team was hot. Texas A&M went in and just absolutely kicked the crap out of them. When I was at South Carolina, we had studied what Texas A&M did, and I explained it to Belichick. He incorporated it into the Giants' game plan. The Giants won, 20–0.

After the game the press was talking to Belichick about what a great defensive game plan he'd had. He said, "I didn't come up with that."

I happened to be walking through the locker room at the time and Belichick pointed to me and said, "He's the one who came up with that." Everybody turned around and said, "Who the hell is that?"

Not only did Belichick use the information, he didn't take the credit for it.

On game day, I would sit in the coaches' booth, next to Al Groh, and chart information for the defense. I would chart everything that happened in the game—the down and distance, the defensive call, the offensive formation, the personnel grouping, and the play. I would give Al the information between defensive series. Then he would relay it to the defensive coaches on the sidelines.

I also would be on a headset that had a switcher that allowed me to listen to the defensive coaches, then switch so that I could answer any questions that Sweatman—who was down on the sidelines—might have on kicking-game situations. You can always see more from the booth than you can from the field. If we were kicking off, Mike might say, "Okay, watch the right side. Tell me who the double's on." Afterward I'd tell him, "They're doubling the three," meaning that the opponent had a double-team block on our third guy lined up from the sideline on our kick-coverage unit. That way, on the next kickoff, we'd know what their scheme was— that they were looking to contain our best cover guy, or maybe they were targeting the spot that their return was going to go.

One of my jobs during practice was to give the defenses to the linebackers who weren't running it on the field. I was around Lawrence Taylor, our great linebacker and one of the greatest players in the history of the game. He played as hard in practice as he did in games. He was a great practice player, which was surprising given how much natural talent he had. I got along great with Taylor and all the linebackers—Carl Banks, Pepper Johnson, Gary Reasons, Steve DeOssie, Johnny Cooks, Bobby Abrams. When you're not in a position of authority, players always treat you great. When you become a person of authority, they don't treat you the same. Talking to your position coach is not the same as talking to the assistant to your position coach. I was just a slappy.

THE FIRST TIME I saw Joe Montana after college was when the Giants played the 49ers during the regular season on *Monday Night Football*. As I walked up to him on the field before our 7–3 loss (which John Taylor decided when he caught a slant pass from Joe and took it to the house), he said, "What are you doing here?"

"I'm coaching," I said.

"For the Giants?"

"Yeah."

"You're shittin' me."

"No."

It was just a quick conversation because Bill didn't like players or coaches fraternizing with the enemy. He would always remind us, "You can talk to them after the game, but don't talk to them before the game. We're going to *play* these guys!"

It's a very simple thought process, but some guys can't help themselves. They want to go find the TV announcers, who are handling the broadcast, as they walk around the field before the game. They want to go up to everyone they see on the field and say, "Hey, how's it going?" I have the same policy as Bill on pregame fraternizing. I'm not as strict about it, but I do always bring it up to the players and coaches.

"Look," I tell them, "we're not into the passing-out-information game."

The next time you go to a football game, just watch the coaching staffs on the field during pregame warm-ups. Just watch who's working it, the conversations between the coaches of the opposing teams. Watch the conversations between the coaches and the players on the other team. You will see that it's rampant.

Of course, having rules about when and how long you could talk to other people was just another way for Bill to exert control over his team. He has always done it that way, and no one does it better. He is a master psychologist. I just love the way Bill controls the psyche of everybody around him. He controls the psyche of the team. He controls the psyche of the media. He's able to manipulate people—and I mean this in a positive, not negative, way—to get them to think, or at least react to the way he thinks. You can talk about Xs and Os with Parcells until you're blue in the face. What separates him from everyone else is how he manages the team.

One of the greatest tactics I learned from Bill is what I call "button pushing." He would make it his business to learn all he could about everyone in his locker room, everyone on his coaching staff, and everyone in every part of the organization. He would find out what made you tick, and then he would find the right buttons to push in order to elevate your performance to a level higher than you ever thought that you could reach. My button was him questioning how hard I worked. I always worked hard, but he would say things like, "So, I see you're trying to get out of here early again, huh?" It never failed. I felt I had to work even harder every time he said that.

Bill did it with everybody. It didn't make any difference whether it was Belichick or Ron Erhardt, our offensive coordinator at the time, or the equipment guys. Everybody was fair game. Bill would find the right button to push. He would play all kinds of mind games.

I would like to think that of all of Bill's qualities that I try to emulate—which are many—the two that stand out the most are his management style and his personality. That personality goes back to both of us being Jersey guys. It's a little gruff. It's sometimes perceived as holier-than-thou, but it really isn't. It's that you've learned that when you're a head coach, you're on an island. You don't have anywhere to go with the problems that come up, not just football problems, but every social issue that you have within a team. You can't go to another head coach, because then you'd be giving away information. You can't go to your assistants, because they aren't the ones leading the team. After a tough loss, there's only one guy who can get the team back on course psychologically, and that's the head coach. The whole team's looking at you. The assistants can lead the guys at their respective positions, but they can't lead the team.

Bill's coaching philosophy with the players was to pressure them hard—stay on them, never relax, never let up. Even when things went well he would still tell his assistant coaches to keep the pressure on. Players never knew where they stood with Bill, and that was exactly how he wanted it. He wanted them uneasy.

The coaches felt that too. He dominated you. You knew he was in control, and there wasn't a damn thing you could do about it. You never sought approval from him, because you weren't going to get it. He would weed out who couldn't handle that. It was his way or the highway.

More players than coaches washed out of his program. Coaches were smart enough to adapt to it, and say, "Okay, that's the way it is." You had no choice if you wanted to work for him, and you wanted to work for him because he was successful.

Bill's football philosophy was simple: Control the ball on

offense and play great defense. The only time he would be more elaborate on offense over the years was when he thought his defense wasn't good. He knew offense, defense, and special teams. His forte was defense, but just like Belichick, those guys who are great defensive coordinators also know the best ways to attack defenses because they know what gives them the most problems.

Belichick and Parcells . . . you don't get any smarter than those two. They're on a different level than most everybody else in this game.

WE FINISHED THE 1990 season with a 13–3 record and won the NFC East. We entered the playoffs without our starting quarterback, Phil Simms, who had already led the Giants to victory in Super Bowl XXI and was the game's MVP. Phil broke his foot in the fourteenth game of the season against Buffalo, and was done for the year. Jeff Hostetler, who until then had been running the show-team offense in practice, took over. Although we wound up losing against the Bills, Jeff did lead us to wins in our final two regular-season games.

In our divisional-round playoff game, we kicked the crap out of the Chicago Bears, 31–3. Hostetler, making his first postseason start, completed only ten passes, but two of them were for touchdowns, and he ran for a third TD. Jeff was an extremely smart guy. Bill and the offensive coaches weren't trying to win the games doing the same things they did with Phil, who was a pocket passer. They moved Jeff around a lot more and tried to do the things he could do best, such as make plays on the run.

Our opponent in the NFC Championship Game was the 49ers, who had won the previous two Super Bowls. We would have to face them at Candlestick Park in San Francisco. In the meantime, because there would be no extra week between the conference championship games and the Super Bowl, we had already broken down all of the videotape of the Bills and the Oakland Raiders—who were playing the same day for the AFC title—so that we would be ready for either of them in Super Bowl XXV. We also packed for two weeks and two destinations: San Francisco and, hopefully, Tampa for the Super Bowl.

The 49ers looked like they might be on their way to a third straight Super Bowl after Joe Montana hooked up with John Taylor for a sixty-one-yard touchdown to give San Francisco a 13–6 lead in the third quarter. We fought back, with Matt Bahr's right foot producing all of our points.

One of the biggest plays of the game was a fake punt. Gary Reasons, one of our linebackers, took a direct snap and ran for thirty yards, which was about as far as he could run before needing oxygen. Sweatman had put the play in the special-teams game plan, but Parcells was the one who called it. The best part about it was, as a bonus, the 49ers had only ten men on the field. The play helped set up Bahr's fourth field goal to cut San Francisco's lead to 13–12 midway through the fourth quarter.

Then Eric Howard put a crushing hit on Roger Craig to force a fumble. Lawrence Taylor recovered with a little more than two minutes left. With the clock winding down, Matt lined up what would be his fifth field goal of the day, from forty-two yards. Upstairs, all we could do was watch. In that situation there's not a damn thing you can do. Sure enough Matt put it through as time expired to give us a 15–13 victory. I'll never forget watching our team photographer signaling that the kick was good as he ran from behind the goal post. We were going to the Super Bowl.

Montana ended up getting hurt badly on a hit by Leonard Marshall. Joe left the game and never returned. I went to see him in the 49ers' locker room after the game. He was still in a daze.

The 49ers were so sure that they were going to win, they had already moved an advance staff into the hotel that would be housing the NFC team for Super Bowl XXV. They were actually moving out when we got there.

We weren't worried about going into the Super Bowl with Hostetler at quarterback rather than Simms. Why should we have been? We had won four other games with Jeff, including the NFC Championship Game. There was no reason to think we weren't going to be able to win the Super Bowl with him.

The Gulf War was going on, which created a very tense atmosphere around the game to say the least. Security was at the highest level everywhere. Forget about the hotels. Going through the gates of Tampa Stadium was ridiculous. Even coming in early, it took the teams forever to get through security. Normally, the security guards give you a little pat-down, but this was just short of a strip search. And that was for the teams playing. You could only imagine what it was like for the fans going into the game. Sitting upstairs in our coaches' booth, I saw the Apache helicopters circling overhead throughout the entire game. I didn't know if I felt safe or threatened by their presence.

Once we settled into our seats, though, the only thing on our minds was business. We didn't get caught up in the fact that it was the Super Bowl. That was right in line with Bill's standing order: "Just do your job!"

The Bills came in with Jim Kelly and that explosive, fast-paced, no-huddle offense that they had just used to pummel the Raiders, 51–3. Against us, they didn't do very much scoring. The score was

20–19 as Scott Norwood came out to attempt a field goal for Buffalo with eight seconds showing on the clock.

Upstairs, again, all we could do was watch. Norwood would be kicking from forty-seven yards . . . on grass. We knew that he had never made a field goal from that distance on grass in the NFL, and had missed his longest previous attempt on grass, from forty-two yards, during the regular season. He kicked it long enough. Luckily for us, it never hooked and wound up sailing wide right.

The most helpless feeling wasn't watching Norwood line up the kick. It was after he missed it, when all of us in the coaches' booth were trying to get down to the field to be part of the wild celebration with the rest of the team. We got down there, but it took awhile.

I couldn't believe it. My first season in the NFL and I was part of a Super Bowl championship. For me, that was a great deal in more ways than one. Besides getting a diamond ring, each member of the coaching staff received sixty-four thousand dollars, which was our share for winning the Super Bowl. That's a lot of money, and it was an especially large sum for me at that time.

Bill ended up having a private party after the game for about a hundred people. At about three-thirty in the morning, I went up to him, slapped him on the back, and said, "I thought you said this was tough."

It was probably the only time that you could ever get away with saying something like that to him.

6

Anyone Want Half a Chicken Sandwich?

Bill Parcells ruled the sidelines during my first stint with New England.

(Photograph by Bert Lane)

"Number one, teach the players what to do.

Number two, always tell the players the truth.

Number three, never try to be the players' friend."

—Ottis "O.J." Anderson,
former Giants running back

At the end of the 1990 season, Bill Parcells retired and took an NFL studio-analyst position with NBC Sports. His replacement was Ray Handley, who had coached running backs for the Giants.

I took Handley's place as running backs coach. That made it easy for me because the man in charge is always going to have the most input at the position he formerly guided. Ray was a very good running backs coach, so I always had him as a resource as far as teaching the fundamentals and techniques of the position. Ray, who had Jim Fassel as his offensive coordinator, also preferred having a young guy like me in the job because he wouldn't have to worry about stepping on my toes or hurting my feelings by saying something. We weren't going to have any philosophical clashes

about how to coach the running backs. We both knew we were going to do it his way.

Ray hired me as a position coach probably before I was justified
in getting a job like that in the NFL. I had just been a quality-
control coach and special-teams assistant coach for one year. Now
I was the running backs coach for the New York Giants. It wasn't
that I thought I was over my head or questioned whether I would be
any good at it. It was just that it was a little early in my career to
have such a big responsibility. I knew that I'd been given another
break. Bill hiring me was one break. Ray making me the running
backs coach was another.

How many breaks can somebody get?

Well, here's one more: I met the woman who would be my wife
at the Jersey Shore on March 9, 1991. I know that this isn't going to
sound very romantic, but the thing that brought us together was a
sandwich—to be precise, half of a chicken sandwich.

We were in a little pub called Leggett's. Maura was there with
three of her friends, two girls and a guy. I was there with one of
my friends, Mike Murphy, a big guy who worked security for the
Giants.

Maura and her friends had just finished eating. She'd only eaten
half of her chicken sandwich; she was planning to bring home the
other half to her dog. Without an invitation, Mike walked over to
their table, picked up Maura's leftover, and ate it. Guess what?
Maura and her friends weren't too happy about that.

I walked to their table to try and smooth things over. Not sur-
prisingly, I wound up taking a verbal beating from Maura and her
friends just for saying that I was with Mike, and it got even worse
when I suggested that he be forgiven for what he'd done. To this
day, they think it was a good-cop/bad-cop situation just so that I

would have the chance to meet Maura. I wish I could say that we were that clever, but I swear it was not orchestrated. Our encounter happened for two simple reasons: Mike had probably had a few beers too many . . . and he was hungry.

I fell in love with Maura the moment I saw her. I don't know if she felt that way about me, but I was determined to start dating her. Until then, I hadn't been looking to date anyone. I had too much work to do. I wanted to move up the ladder in the coaching profession. I aspired to be excellent at what I was doing, and I thought that dating someone would be a distraction. Maura definitely was the exception to the rule, but I had to work on her. I figured the best way to start was to talk with everyone at the table rather than just to her.

After about an hour one of her friends, Lisa, who was a big Giants fan, asked me, "So what do you do?"

"I coach football," I said.

"Pop Warner?"

"No."

"High school?"

"No."

"College?"

"No."

"Well, the next thing you're going to do is tell me you coach for the Giants."

"Well, as a matter of fact, I do."

"You do not. I know every one of those guys."

"Well, that's what I do."

"Prove it."

I pulled one of my business cards out of my wallet and handed it to her. She wasn't impressed.

"Anyone could have these made," she said.

The next day Lisa did a little investigating. When she saw Maura, she told her, "He wasn't lying. He really does coach for the Giants."

"Big deal," Maura said.

Maura, who lived on the Jersey Shore and worked in sales for a company called Applause that sold products to merchants along the boardwalk, did not follow football. She was born in Manhattan, but spent a good portion of her life in Staten Island, where she started riding horses at thirteen. Horse people don't care about too many other sports. They just care about horses. All Maura knew about football was that the Giants had won the Super Bowl and that Bill Parcells was their coach. If you knew nothing else about the Giants, you knew those two things.

I had gotten Maura's phone number and the following night, I invited all four of them who had been at the table out to dinner later in the week because I knew I wasn't going to get anywhere asking just Maura. Now that they knew that I wasn't lying, they came around to accepting my invitation. At dinner we talked about a bunch of things. Then someone asked me, "How did you get this coaching job with the Giants?"

"I prayed a lot," I said. "I made a deal with God that if He would just give me this job, it would be the only thing I'd ever pray for for myself, personally. He came through for me, so I've used up all of my prayers."

Maura told me later that night that she liked the fact that, sitting at a table with four people I didn't know, I was giving thanks to God for the biggest break of my career. That dinner was the turning point of our relationship. Before then, I was just the guy who was with that other guy who had eaten half of her chicken sandwich. Afterward her opinion of me became more favorable. We started dating.

We were both in our thirties, so we weren't kids. I bought a house in August of that year, and she moved in with me in the fall. One of the reasons I wanted us to start living together then was to let her see what being with me during football season was all about—to see whether she could handle it—because this was what I was going to continue to do for a living. I was putting in a lot of hours, and I wanted her to experience that.

It didn't discourage her. We got engaged on October 16, 1991, and were married on June 21, 1992.

Maura is the one person in this world who knows me, understands me, and loves me unconditionally, realizing that I have many faults. I trust her more than anyone.

Now the woman who once didn't care that I was an assistant coach for the Giants is a football expert. Ironically, a lot of the friends Maura grew up with were die-hard sports fans. If they had any clue what path her life has taken since 1990, they'd never believe it. I'm sure that if any of them ran into her at a high-school reunion or anywhere else, they'd say, "You're the wife of a football coach?"

To Maura's credit, she has shared a critical football opinion with me only once. It happened just before the '91 season, while we were still dating. As the Giants went through training camp that summer, Handley was going to decide whether Jeff Hostetler, who had just helped us win a Super Bowl, or Phil Simms, whose injury had opened the door for Hostetler, would be the starting quarterback. We finally announced it was going to be Hostetler. I went home that day and Maura said, "You picked Hostetler over Simms?"

"Honey, I have to listen to this all day long," I said. "I'm not listening to it when I come home."

Fortunately, that was the last time we ever had that sort of conversation.

The previous year, under Parcells, Handley had signaled the plays from the sidelines to the quarterback. Now it was my turn. This was prior to the electronic coach-to-quarterback communication system, so we worked with hand signals to relay the plays from the game plan that the offensive staff put together.

I would meet with the quarterbacks and create an intricate signaling system, then practice those signals with them multiple times in a week. If a play was run from only one formation, they would have to memorize that formation to abbreviate the signal. If a play was run from multiple formations, the formation would be signaled as well as the play. Sometimes we would run one play from more than ten formations.

A prime example was a play we used to call "Ride Thirty-four," which was an inside zone running play. We would use different personnel groups and wide receiver motions to disguise the look of the play, but the play was still the same.

Saturday mornings would be especially enjoyable for me. We would give a signal test, and Simms and Hostetler would compete to see who could get the most right. The way they competed, you would have thought it was the Super Bowl.

THE BEST COACHING advice I ever received didn't come from Parcells, Belichick, or any coach for that matter. It came from my starting halfback, Ottis "O.J." Anderson, who was the MVP of Super Bowl XXV. O.J. and my starting fullback, Maurice Carthon, who is now the offensive coordinator of the Browns, were almost my age.

"You know, Charlie, you're going to be a great leader and a great coach, but let me give you three bits of advice," O.J. said one day. "Number one, teach the players what to do; don't assume they already know what to do. Number two, always tell the players the truth, regardless of the consequences. Number three, never try to be the players' friend.

"Those are the three things that make the difference between coaches succeeding or failing."

Since then, I have always tried to live by those principles. If you can't be brutally honest with your players, if you're worried about hurting their feelings, then you have no chance. When you're a leader, you can't be buddy-buddy with the people that play for you, because you're the same one that's going to have to get all over them when things aren't going so well. With our players and assistant coaches, I don't try to be their friend. I try to be their boss.

After going 8–8 in 1991 and 6–10 in 1992, Ray Handley was fired and would be replaced by Dan Reeves. At the same time, Parcells came out of retirement to take over as head coach of the Patriots in 1993. Bill offered me a job coaching tight ends, which I accepted, because he had already hired Dave Atkins from Philadelphia to be his running backs coach. Ray Perkins, a former head coach of the Giants, would be the offensive coordinator.

A little more than a month after I took the job with the Patriots, I ran into Reeves at the NFL Scouting Combine in Indianapolis. He had gone to the University of South Carolina, and a lot of his former teammates had been friends of Coach Morrison's. They all loved me from my time there and had kept encouraging Reeves to keep me on the Giants' staff.

"You never gave me an opportunity to even talk to you," Reeves said.

I appreciated that he mentioned that, but even if we had talked, I would still have gone with Parcells because I was familiar with him and all aspects of his coaching and football philosophies, and because I felt loyal to the guy who had given me my first job in the NFL.

Maura was pregnant with Charlie when Handley was fired from the Giants. A little more than a month later, there was a nor'easter. Although Maura was in her eighth month, she drove through the blizzard to join me in Foxboro and deal with all of the stuff that needed to be done for our move, including lining up a doctor to deliver our first child. Charlie was born on April 29, 1993.

When I arrived in New England, it was not a great situation. The Patriots were coming off a 2–14 season under Dick MacPherson. Their owner was James Orthwein, a St. Louis businessman who bought the team in 1992 and wanted to move it to St. Louis. The only thing stopping him was Robert Kraft, a native of Brookline, Massachusetts, and the owner of what was then known as Sullivan Stadium, named after the founder of the franchise, Billy Sullivan. Kraft wouldn't let Orthwein out of his stadium lease. Kraft eventually bought the team to make sure it stayed in New England.

He also would bring much-needed improvements to the organization, but that would take some time. Back then, the Patriots had a no-frills operation, although when Parcells came in they sold a bunch of tickets, and when they made Drew Bledsoe, a quarterback from Washington State, the top overall pick of the '93 draft they sold a bunch more.

The stadium was a dump. The locker rooms were small. You never knew if you were going to have hot water or not. You never knew if a pipe was going to break, and if one did, you didn't know who was going to fix it. Just trying to keep the place serviceable was a struggle. It was a significant step down from what I had been around with the Giants.

WE MADE A little improvement on the field that first year, finishing 5–11. I had the opportunity to work with two very good tight ends—Marv Cook, a fifth-year veteran and Pro Bowler, and a talented third-year guy named Ben Coates. Marv started twelve games for us in '93 and ended up catching twenty-two passes. Ben made only four starts, but led the team with fifty-three receptions and had our second-longest catch that year on a fifty-four-yard touchdown. The difference between them was that Marv was a short-to-intermediate receiver, whereas Ben was more of a three-level receiver—short, intermediate, and deep. We threw a number of deep balls to Ben.

Standing six feet five inches, Coates was a long strider. Long striders usually aren't very fast, but when Ben got going, he'd run faster. Long striders also tend to have problems with the short-to-intermediate routes because it's harder for them to get in and out of breaks than it is for someone with shorter legs, but Ben learned how to use his body to get open. He would push off and rarely get penalized by the officials for doing it. He also had very dependable hands. He clicked with Bledsoe, and Drew would always look to him.

After Ben took over as the starting tight end in 1994, his catches skyrocketed to ninety-six, which at the time was the most by any tight end in NFL history. He made the first of many Pro Bowls. That isn't coaching. That's chemistry.

After our 10–6 finish in '94 (and first-round playoff loss to Cleveland), I was just starting to feel good about myself as a tight ends coach. Then, in 1995, Parcells moved Mike Pope, who had been our running backs coach, to tight ends coach and gave me the running backs.

At that point, Charlie was two years old and Maura was pregnant with Hannah. Six and a half months into the pregnancy, during an ultrasound examination, an abnormality was found in Hannah's kidneys.

After that, we went to the New England Medical Center in Boston, where Hannah was diagnosed with infantile polycystic kidney disease. Without going into the whole description of what it is, the important thing to know is that it's basically a fatal disease and that there was a good chance that Hannah was dying before she was born. The doctors told us that one of our options was to abort the baby, which was not an option for us.

Every Friday morning that spring, Maura and I had to drive into Boston so doctors could check Maura's amniotic fluid to see if Hannah was alive. Although it was the off-season and there wasn't much going on, I still felt guilty about leaving the office. I asked Bill for permission, and without hesitation he said, "Go."

Each week, the amniotic fluid levels checked out fine. After the examination, I'd drop Maura off at home, then go to work. Bill would always ask, "How did it go?" I was always happy to tell him, "Fine."

Although Hannah had problems, the diagnosis proved to be wrong. Hannah was born on April 7, 1995. Going through that was brutal for both of us. I was just feeling it emotionally. Maura was living it *and* feeling it. She was a trooper. She's one tough Irish Catholic.

We weren't completely out of the woods, though. Two months later, Hannah underwent surgery for the removal of her right kidney and to have her left ureter, a tube that connects the kidney to the bladder, reimplanted in the bladder to fix a blockage.

The whole ordeal was tough. It was miserable, but you always have to be able to separate work from family. If you're any good at your profession, that's what you have to do.

WHILE ALL OF that was going on with Hannah, we were getting ready for the 1995 draft. Running back, the position I was now coaching, was our biggest need, and we used a third-round pick on a junior from the University of Pittsburgh named Curtis Martin.

A lot of people don't realize that Curtis was a gift for us. He had played only one game and one quarter of his junior year. In his first game, against Texas, he ran the ball up and down the field. The next game, against Ohio University, he suffered a high ankle sprain at the end of the first quarter, but he had already rushed for about a hundred yards.

Curtis thought he was healthy enough to play later in his junior year, but the coaches at Pittsburgh wanted to medically redshirt him. He felt that they were just trying to keep him there an extra season to serve their own interests, so he declared himself eligible for the draft.

Maurice Carthon, whom I coached on the Giants and who now was our assistant running backs coach, worked Curtis out on the Pitt campus and came back and said he was absolutely phenomenal. We had Curtis rated as a starting running back in the league right out of college. As we approached the third round, we talked about trading the pick for multiple choices, but instead we took

Curtis—and we were certainly glad we did. Although we ended up going 6–10 in 1995, Curtis rushed for nearly fifteen hundred yards, scored fourteen rushing touchdowns, and went to the Pro Bowl.

At the end of the '95 season, Parcells hired Belichick, who had spent the previous five seasons as head coach of the Browns, as assistant head coach–secondary coach. Parcells promoted Carthon to running backs coach and made Chris Palmer, who had been our receivers coach, the quarterbacks coach. And he moved me to yet another new position—receivers.

Sure enough, in the 1996 draft, we used our first-round pick on a receiver, Terry Glenn, from Ohio State. Terry had a lot of ability—speed, quickness, hands. I just needed to help him develop his knowledge of the game, such as being a dependable route runner, and help him get the confidence he needed to do it. It wasn't anything athletic that I was honing, but off-field things. This was a smart kid, but he was young. Like Martin, he entered the league as an underclassman, and had been only a one-year starter in college.

One of Terry's biggest adjustments was learning how to deal with Parcells's button pushing. When Terry missed a preseason game because of a hamstring strain, Bill referred to him as "she," which caused some hard feelings on Terry's part. I had to do some massaging with that relationship. I was like the intermediary. I even had the kid come over to my house. I don't normally get close with players, but in this case I wanted to do my best to make sure there wasn't a volatile relationship between Bill and Terry.

Terry wasn't a great practice player, which didn't fit well with Bill's mentality, but he always showed up on Sundays. That was the bottom line. He caught ninety balls as a rookie to help us finish 11–5, win the AFC East, and reach Super Bowl XXXI, in New Orleans, where we would face the Green Bay Packers.

There were two weeks between the AFC Championship Game, in which we beat Jacksonville, and the Super Bowl, so it was totally different from the first one I experienced, with the Giants. There were all sorts of rumors about Parcells leaving for the Jets. None of us on the coaching staff found that to be a distraction, since Bill wasn't telling us that he was leaving. We just focused on our jobs, which was to get the team ready to play in the Super Bowl.

Unfortunately, we didn't do a good enough job of that, and we lost, 35–21.

The rumors about Bill Parcells proved to be true. He was taking the Jets' job in place of Rich Kotite. It was assumed that Bill Belichick would replace him in New England, but Robert Kraft decided to hire Pete Carroll, who had been the Jets' head coach before Kotite, instead.

Several of us from the Patriots' staff went along with Parcells, and several others—including Palmer, who left for Jacksonville to become Tom Coughlin's offensive coordinator—did not. We had a pretty big challenge in front of us. The Jets had finished 1–15 the previous year, the worst record in the NFL. We had only one direction to go.

Given what we had done in New England, I was confident we could get the Jets moving in the right direction as well.

7

With Life and Game Plans, Always Prepare for Something Else

Feeling good, ready—but always prepared for changes—
with my call sheet. *(Courtesy of the New York Jets)*

People look at kids with special needs and say, "What's wrong with them?" My response: "It's not their fault."

Maura and I have been through a lot together. Most of our trials and tribulations have stemmed from our daughter, Hannah, and from the job changes and resulting moves that are typical in the world of football coaching. We moved to Northport, Long Island, to be near the Jets' practice facility in Hempstead. Up to that point, Hannah had been a happy baby, apparently thriving, even though we were still learning and worrying about how she was going to be able to survive with one kidney.

Around her second birthday, we started to notice a different set of problems with her, although we didn't know exactly what they were. She seemed to go into a fog. At first we waited for her to come out of it. Maura and I said, "Oh, we're just a little slow, we're just a little delayed. Everything will be better."

We took her to a neurologist, went to every type of doctor known to man. After one year on Long Island, our never-ending search for the best care for Hannah took us back to New Jersey and, once again, to a home at the Shore—an eighty-eight-mile drive to Hempstead, one way.

Hannah was eventually diagnosed with pervasive development disorder (PDD), which comes under the umbrella of autism. From that time until today, at age eleven, she has seen close to a hundred doctors who have diagnosed different things that have been wrong with her. She has severe global developmental delays—which is the modern-day vernacular for mental retardation—and there are several problems that come along with that. One is that she needs to take medication to keep her from having multiple miniseizures. She also has severe food allergies, although one benefit of that is she follows a healthy diet because there is a lot of stuff she can't eat.

As a parent, you start out feeling sorry for yourself, and that was exactly what we did. Why me? Why did it have to happen to us? It wasn't as if Maura or I had done anything wrong. We didn't drink, smoke, or do drugs. One theory is that Hannah, like many other children with forms of autism, could have gotten it from a measles-mumps-rubella vaccine containing mercury. That has not been scientifically proven.

Do I wish Hannah were a perfectly normal kid? Absolutely. She's not; she will always have problems. But she's also happy. That's the catch-22. Hannah's not very verbal, but sometimes she'll walk up to somebody either on the playground or on the beach and say, "Hi." Some people respond, "Eeew! Eeew! Get away from me." Sometimes we'd go into a grocery store and, all of a sudden, Hannah would have one of her fits—which don't happen very often anymore—and people would stare her down as if to say, "Eeew! Go away." That's disheartening because they don't understand that this is not some animal. This is your daughter.

People both lack awareness of and show little compassion for kids with special needs. They say, "What's wrong with them?" My response: "It's not their fault."

Eventually, you get past that self-pity phase and get past the anger phase. When you realize it's a permanent problem and not temporary, you say, "Okay, now what are we going to do about it?"

We're trying to turn a negative into a positive. In the spring of 2003, my wife and I set up a charity called Hannah and Friends. Besides raising money for children with special needs, we've given out, through a program called Hannah's Helping Hands, hundreds of grants to people with special needs from disadvantaged families. In addition to that, we're planning to build a complex for adults with special needs in the South Bend area. We're looking to have this project done before Hannah turns eighteen.

The biggest fear of any parent with a kid with special needs is, What happens if we're gone? We think that we can help a lot more of these special-needs kids who become special-needs adults. You can't just shun them when they're thirty-five. You don't just throw them away. You have to find a way to let them be happy in life. Not only did we confront the problems with Hannah, but we've used that experience to help more and more people all the time. We feel pretty good about that.

Here's how I like to describe my family: I call Maura my best friend, I call Charlie my best buddy, and I call Hannah our guiding angel. This might sound corny, but my wife and I believe God sent Hannah down as a messenger for us to do some good. One of the reasons I'm so committed to the charity work for Hannah and Friends is because I believe that's why Hannah is here.

At the same time, we have to make sure we don't shun our son. His only sibling has special needs, and that has been rough on Charlie. He's a very sensitive boy, but he's a very good boy. When he left Mercymount Country Day, the school he attended in Cumberland, Rhode Island, for five years while I was with the Patriots, the principal told me that in twenty years she had never had a nicer boy than Charlie as a student. He is polite, he's a gentleman, and he can communicate with adults.

Charlie and I have a ritual that goes back to when he was three or four and started having nightmares that woke him in the middle of the night and sent him running into our bedroom. Every night before he goes to sleep, I say the same three things: "You're my best buddy, I love you very much, and sweet dreams and good luck." The "good luck" wish is to get through the night without having any nightmares.

Sometimes now, when he's around his friends and doesn't want either of us to say it out loud because it wouldn't be cool, he'll just say, "Dad, three things?"

"Right, Charlie," I'll say. "Three things."

WHEN WE GOT to the Jets in 1997, Parcells was going to become more involved in the offense, so he wanted somebody to run the offense who would be comfortable in a situation where he could interject his thoughts whenever he wanted. Ron Erhardt—who had been with the Jets the previous season when Rich Kotite was head coach—was Parcells's biggest advocate and an experienced offensive coordinator. However, Ron would not have been perfect for that kind of role. An old-school guy, Ron wanted to run the offense his way without any interference from the head coach.

Bill told me in training camp that he wanted to try me out as the play caller through preseason and see how it went. It went pretty well, even though, officially, I was still listed only as the wide receivers coach. Bill didn't want to make the play-calling role public for two reasons: one, he wanted to protect me in case things went bad; two, he didn't want to put Ron into a bad situation by having a guy of his caliber on the staff and then bringing a younger guy in to be the play caller.

The only glitch I had that summer was in training-camp practices. I didn't know it at the time, but our defensive coaches were taking copies of the plays we were going to run on offense and going over them in meetings with their players before each practice. That gave the defense an unfair edge once we got on the field. It took a while for me to figure out, and shame on me for letting them take advantage of my naïveté. (In the following year's training camp, I was much more careful about who got to see the actual plays that we were installing on offense. At the same time, I put together a fake list of plays that I was not so careful about hiding, so the defense would start copying plays we weren't even putting in. That turned the tables in practice.)

The major part of my new duties was designing the offensive game plan. Although I had never done that before, I thought I could handle the job. The process of putting together the game plan was pretty basic: I did the research, used the input from the whole staff, and then got Bill to rubber-stamp it.

Bill had confidence that I could design a game plan that he would both know and understand. For a head coach whose forte is defense, having somebody he can trust to do all of the research and establish an offensive game plan where he can understand both what's being done and why makes his job much easier. My job was made easy by the fact that if Bill wanted to call something in a game, he could. I would just set up the call sheet and start calling the game, and whenever Bill said, "I want to run this," I ran it. Simple.

What I knew about designing an offense went all the way back to my days with the Giants. Ron Erhardt, Ray Handley, Jim Fassel, Ray Perkins, Chris Palmer, Mike Pope, Mo Carthon (who came with Parcells to be the Jets' running backs coach), Freddy Hoaglin (who had been an offensive line coach with the Giants and Patriots), Bill Muir (who was the offensive line coach with the Jets when we got there), and Pat Hodgson (who was the tight ends coach with the Jets when we got there) all influenced me. We had a lot of different, contrasting personalities, but everyone could get on the same page for a game and understand what we were doing and why. With the Giants and the Patriots, I had been part of two very good, meticulous staffs. All I did was follow the formula.

Everyone has his role when it comes to researching an opponent so you have the least amount of wasted time with the greatest amount of productivity. I think there are many teams where the whole offensive staff sits together for everything the offense is preparing to do in a game plan. The problem with that approach is that coaches end up sitting in on discussions about different parts of the game plan that don't involve them, so they don't care about what is being said.

So rather than have them involved in the whole process, you let them research the areas that they know best. For instance, when it comes to the run game, you're more inclined to listen to your offensive line coach, your running backs coach, and your tight ends coach, whereas in the pass game you're more inclined to listen to your quarterbacks coach and your receivers coach. It all depends on what you are dealing with. I also seek the input of the defensive coaches to hear what ideas they might have about the most effective strategy against some of the things they do on defense.

FROM MY TIME with the Giants and New England, I learned never to forget that football comes down to a personnel game. I've always understood that as well as, if not better than, everyone else. Whereas other offensive coordinators just worried about Xs and Os and drawing up plays, my forte was hiding the weaknesses that we had and attacking the weaknesses that they had. Part of it was schematics, which comes from research, but a big part of it was knowing the personnel on both sides of the ball.

If you're going against a middle linebacker who excels as a run stopper, then you play-action and throw over the top of him all game long. He'll never make a play, because with the play-action, he'll always be looking to stop the run, and you'll always be able to exploit that by throwing behind him.

If you have an offensive tackle who is a bit stiff athletically, you can't hang him out to dry by isolating him one-on-one with a defensive end and letting him just get beat the whole game. You've got to either slide another lineman over to give him help or give him help with a back or a tight end. Very seldom can you help both tackles. To help both tackles you have to keep seven men in. Usually, with one tackle, you say, "He can handle his guy; we'll help the other guy." Very few teams have two defensive ends that you're concerned about. When they do, you have a problem.

I have always memorized the call sheet before each game, even though I carry a laminated copy of it with me on the sidelines. Each play is numbered with the formation. Passes are in blue, runs are in green, red-zone plays are in red. If a play's not on that sheet, we're usually not calling it. Every once in a while, we'll draw one up in the dirt.

With the Jets, we never had to worry about anyone stealing our signals because we never signaled. If the coach-to-quarterback communication system went down, we just had to give the number of the play, which changed for each game. The quarterback looked at his wristband, with all of the plays and corresponding numbers on it, and made the call.

My first regular-season game calling plays for the Jets, on August 31, 1997, was a big game for me. We went to the Kingdome to play the Seattle Seahawks. We were supposed to get smoked in that game. The oddsmakers had us somewhere around a ten-point underdog. Neil O'Donnell threw five touchdown passes and we kicked their butt, 41–3. In the first half it seemed like we scored every time we got the ball. We just went up and down the field on them. The Seahawks were supposed to be a halfway decent team, and it was a massacre.

In the opener, you can always attack schemes because you've had the whole off-season to prepare. We thought we had some ways to get after them, and almost everything worked. It was never announced that I was the play caller and designer. Everyone assumed it was Erhardt. In fact, after that Seattle game, reporters went up to Neil and said, "Ron called a great game."

"Ron didn't call the game," Neil said. "Charlie called the game."

That was the first time anyone got any inkling about it, although the story didn't go much beyond that because Bill didn't discuss it and didn't allow the coaching staff to talk with the media.

We ended up going 9–7 in that '97 season. We missed the play-offs after losing to Detroit by a field goal in the last game of the year. Shortly thereafter, Erhardt retired. Bill hired Dan Henning to be the quarterbacks coach and officially made me the offensive coordinator. I didn't have the experience that Dan had, but once again, Bill knew that a veteran coach wouldn't be as comfortable as I was working in a situation where the head coach would be interjecting his thoughts in the offense.

I will say this about Ron and Dan: even though they had been head coaches and coordinators a lot longer than I had, they were very supportive and helpful.

THERE WERE GAMES when Parcells would call most of the plays, and there were games when he wouldn't call many. I had to be ready, from game to game, to feed him the plays to call or to call them myself.

I always prepared the call sheet as if I were going to be the one calling the plays and then went over it with Bill the day before the game. If Bill believed he had a feel for how to beat a particular team, then he was going to handle the play calling, whether he called all the plays or took over during the game. It could happen at any time. The only time Bill wouldn't get involved with calling plays was on those rare occasions when he felt really uncomfortable with the team we were going against.

People made a big deal when it came out in the media that Bill took over the play calling from me in one game, but it had been that way from Day One. He was the boss, so if that was what he wanted, guess what? He won.

Was I happy? No, because I never went into a game certain how it was going to play out. The best part of the uncertainty, though, was that it forced me to prepare even more for each game because I never knew who was going to call the plays. I had to make sure, with everything I had on the sheet, that I was not thinking just the way I would think. I had to be thinking the way he would think too.

For instance, I might think the best way to attack an opponent was to go with an empty backfield and throw on every down because they couldn't cover anybody. Bill might say, "The hell with that. We're going to pound 'em with running plays."

After we signed Curtis Martin as a restricted free agent in 1998, that was often a good way to go. He rushed for nearly 1,300 yards in his first season with the Jets, and a year later he ran for 1,464 yards. That was a team record that he would eventually break on the way to establishing himself as the franchise's all-time leading rusher. Curtis was as good as, if not better than, any running back I've ever been around. He had great vision, great instincts, great hands, and great toughness.

In the same game plan, we'd have both empty and pound-'em plays even though we might end up calling the pound-'em plays he wanted and none of the empty ones I wanted. In another game it might be just the opposite: I might be thinking the best way of doing it is to pound 'em, and he might be saying, "No, the best way in this game is to throw it."

Either way, it was all in the game plan. Regardless of what the defense showed us or how we might have been executing in one phase or another, we had an answer. That's the most important thing—to have an answer. A lot of coaches go into games and don't have an answer if something doesn't work. How many games have you seen where one offense keeps doing something that obviously isn't working? I'm not one of those coaches. If something isn't working, I won't keep doing it long. I'm not waiting until halftime to fix it. Not that Bill planned on doing this, but he created an environment for me to learn the importance of having more potential answers in case something doesn't work.

Not that he planned on doing this, either, but he also created an environment that helped me learn how to suppress my ego. The biggest weakness of any young coach is an overinflated ego. Everyone wants to be the next coming of Knute Rockne, the next Vince Lombardi, and you think you're going to be the one. Every young coach has a tendency to either openly or discreetly self-promote, and I was no exception. When you finally grow up, when you're more concerned with figuring out a way to win than with making sure that everyone knows who you are and what contributions you've made, then you've taken it to the level that very few people reach in this business.

For me that happened because of how the play calling went down with Parcells, not in spite of it.

The one decision that Parcells and—later, when I returned to New England—Bill Belichick always made when I was calling plays for them was whether to go for it on fourth down. You go into a game with preconceived notions of when you're going to go for it and when you're not. Sometimes the decision's dictated by field position. Sometimes it's dictated by the defense you're playing against. Sometimes it's dictated by weather, especially when you decide to go for it on fourth down rather than kick a field goal.

Let's say it's fourth-and-one, you're outside the opponent's 30-yard line, and you're going against the wind. If you punt you could have a touchback and end up with a net difference in field position of ten yards. If the wind is so strong that you think you can't make the field goal, that's a prime time to go for it. A layman might look at the decision and say, "Why didn't they kick the field goal?" It was because we'd already decided that we couldn't make the field goal because of the wind.

I consider myself an educated risk taker. I like to play the odds. You're not right every time, but at least you've put some thought into it rather than just being reckless.

COACHING WIDE RECEIVERS for the Jets was interesting because I had Keyshawn Johnson and Wayne Chrebet right after Keyshawn's book, *Just Give Me the Damn Ball,* had come out. In the book Keyshawn was critical of Wayne, referring to him as "the team's mascot." That was a tension-filled receivers meeting room every day, but I didn't worry about it. I just went ahead and coached them.

I never saw them argue. I never heard them say boo to each other. They might not have liked each other, but they played hard together. On the field, they covered each other's butt. I don't think you'd ever see them going out to dinner together, but they did their jobs well and with a great deal of pride. As a result, each guy benefited from the other's performance.

Following the premise that you go by what you see, rather than what someone else tells you, all I saw from Keyshawn Johnson was one hardworking, competitive player that made plays for us for three years. I have zero complaints about Keyshawn. I've never had a problem with him. When Keyshawn bitched about not being involved in the game plan, I would tell him, "I'm game-planning Tuesday morning. Go watch a bunch of tape, and if you have any thoughts about the game plan based on research you've done, let me know by Monday night."

Sure enough, he would go and watch a half dozen games of

how teams attacked the defense of the upcoming opponent and then call me up and give me some thoughts. We'd be getting ready to play the Dolphins and he'd say, "Go look at the thirty-seventh play of the Buffalo game, Eric Moulds running a route on Sam Madison." I would go look at some of those things early Tuesday morning and then try to incorporate a couple of those ideas into the game plan.

Keyshawn was one of the hardest working guys we had. If I told Keyshawn that he had a weakness, he would stay out after practice and work on it for a half hour. Once he realized that he wasn't going to win all of his routes by his quickness and needed to use his strength, he became a much better player. He learned he could create separation by pushing as well as by running away from someone. I've got nothing bad to say about Keyshawn. He could play for me any day.

Wayne Chrebet was a different kind of player. He was a cult hero when I got to the Jets. He was everyone's All-American. He was the "Rudy" of the Jets, following a path like that of Rudy Ruettiger, the famous Notre Dame walk-on who inspired a movie. Wayne had the classic, feel-good story: Jersey boy . . . goes to Hofstra . . . makes one of the hometown teams as a free-agent walk-on.

However, there was a big difference between Wayne and Rudy. Wayne had plenty of talent. He played up to that "Rudy" image. Wayne loved being in that no-respect mode, but he was as good a slot receiver as you could ever see. He was a money player on third down. You couldn't cover him one-on-one because he was too strong and too quick. He also had great hands. The quarterback would always look to throw to Wayne on third down because he knew that he would have a completion. He didn't look for Wayne as much on first or second down, unless we had three wide receivers in and Wayne was in the slot, but on third down the ball was going to Chrebet.

Neil O'Donnell had a solid year for us at quarterback, but he and Bill didn't get along well at the end of the '97 season, so he left. Glenn Foley was going to be the starter in 1998. We also brought in Vinny Testaverde to give us solid veteran depth. Our opener that year was against San Francisco. Foley threw for four hundred yards and we lost a heartbreaker in overtime. Then Foley got hurt in the second game, Vinny came in, and he played great the rest of the year.

Vinny had a great arm and good touch, and he still had pretty good feet. He could run a lot better than people thought he could. Not that we had a bunch of rollout plays for him, but he was not slow afoot. One thing about Vinny was that he didn't want you to overwhelm him with how much offense you had. I can't tell you how many plays we would throw out of the game plan because Vinny didn't like them.

We'd put the game plan in on Tuesday with about a hundred total plays, including red-area, third-down, and two-minute situations. We'd practice on Wednesday and Thursday, and then Thursday after practice, Vinny would come into my office and we'd throw out anywhere from ten to twenty plays that he did not like. Vinny would say, "I don't like that play," and I'd throw it out even if I loved it. My feelings about the play didn't matter. If the quarterback doesn't have confidence in a play, it's not going to work, because he's the one who has to make it work. Vinny liked plays that you'd run over and over—the kind of plays that, when they were called, he was confident that everyone around him knew what to do.

It was hard to argue with his approach. He brought us to the AFC Championship Game, where we lost to the Denver Broncos.

Vinny popped his Achilles tendon in the 1999 opener against New England, as he was handing off on a counter to Curtis Martin. Considering the other injuries we had that year, that would be one of the rare times when I'd ever say that going 8–8 was a great season.

8 ————

A "Snow Bowl," a Super Bowl . . .
and an Everlasting Spirit

Working with Tommy Brady was the highlight of my NFL
coaching career. *(Photograph by David Silverman)*

"Yeah, I was watching those [Super Bowl come-back highlights] too. Wouldn't it be cool if [Super Bowl XXXVI] came down to something like that?"

—Tom Brady,
Patriots quarterback

After the '99 season, Bill Parcells stepped down as head coach of the Jets and became their director of football operations. That automatically triggered a clause in Bill Belichick's contract making him the new head coach of the Jets.

However, the Patriots wanted Belichick to be their head coach to replace Pete Carroll, and Belichick wanted to take that job. There was a technicality concerning Belichick's contract with the Jets and whether Parcells's resignation could actually prevent Belichick from becoming head coach of the Patriots or any other team besides the Jets. In the end the Jets agreed to let Belichick go to New England—in exchange for three draft picks, including a first-rounder. They promoted Al Groh from linebackers coach to head coach. I ended up going with Belichick to New England as offensive coordinator.

At the same time that Belichick offered me the job with the Patriots, Jim Haslett, then the head coach of the New Orleans Saints, talked with me about being his coordinator. Jim didn't even know me. He said, "I've talked with ten guys around the league, and they all tell me I should hire you." I appreciated hearing that. I thanked him, but said I would be going with Belichick. If it hadn't been for Belichick stepping up during the contract negotiations, I might have been with the Saints.

Like Parcells, Belichick was a button pusher. Like Parcells, he knew where those buttons were, and when and how to press them to get the most out of his players and staff.

I've always felt that his greatest asset, though, was his insight and foresight into today's football. By insight, I mean that on a week-to-week basis, he could dissect the game—through an analytical approach using all of the computer-age technology at his disposal—as well as or better than anyone I know. By foresight, I mean that he always seemed able to look a year or two years or three years down the road and head off issues—whether they were personnel issues or salary-cap issues—before they became problems.

As a head coach, I would like to think that I have both of those traits. I would like to think that I'm thinking along the lines of both Bills in my approach, especially when it comes to putting the team ahead of the individual. It's not that I have all kinds of notes that I refer to about them, because I didn't take any. Some guys would write down everything they said. For me, it was just a case of absorbing what I saw and heard during all of the years I spent around them.

I do the exact same stuff they do. It's all plagiarizing. Here's an example to illustrate the point: the Patriots picked up three players from our 2005 Notre Dame team—offensive guard Dan Stevenson as a sixth-round pick in the 2006 draft, wide receiver Matt Shelton, and linebacker Corey Mays, the latter two signing as free agents. During their minicamp right after the draft, I spoke with Belichick on the phone.

"Every time I say something, the Notre Dame guys are all laughing," Belichick said. "They told me, 'We've heard all this stuff before.'"

That's right. They heard it from me . . . after I heard it from Belichick . . . after he heard it from Parcells. Now they're hearing it from Belichick again, completing the circle of football gospel that stands the test of time.

THE SITUATION WHEN I returned to New England was totally different from my previous stint there. When I arrived with Parcells in '93, the Patriots were coming off a 2–14 season. In 2000, we inherited an 8–8 team. We had less distance to make up, but it still felt like we had a long way to go before this would be a Super Bowl–caliber team.

Another big difference from my first time with the Patriots was that I was the head coach's offensive right-hand man. That didn't mean Belichick would not interject his opinion, but he was counting on me to run the offense. Now I was the guy who was supposed to be in charge of half the team, while still being under the guidance of the head coach.

Drew Bledsoe had grown up a lot as a quarterback. Remember, when we drafted him seven years earlier, he was a twenty-one-year-old junior in college. Now, he was a married man with two of his eventual four kids.

Drew was embedded as the starter, but we were still planning to draft a quarterback that year. Belichick and Scott Pioli, our vice president of player personnel, had narrowed down to three the quarterbacks they would be interested in on the second day of the 2000 draft. They had Dick Rehbein, our quarterbacks coach, study each of the three prospects on videotape. The one Dick liked best was the same one they liked best: Tom Brady of Michigan. We drafted him in the sixth round.

Where we selected Tommy didn't matter to us in terms of the potential we thought he had to eventually become our starter. The way we looked at it, a sixth-round draft choice could just as well be a first-round draft choice. The round didn't mean anything to us.

It did mean something to Tommy, though. He came in with a little bit of a chip on his shoulder because he thought that he was a lot better than everyone in the NFL thought he was at the time. Robert Kraft told me later that Tommy had told him he was going to prove to be the best draft pick the Patriots ever made.

You could see that Tommy just had something special about him. We liked his moxie and his intelligence. He was kind of skinny at the time. It didn't take a brain surgeon to figure out that he needed to put on some weight and gain some muscle.

We weren't counting on him to play his rookie year, so he didn't have that pressure on him. We decided we were going to keep him as a fourth quarterback—behind Drew, John Friesz, and Michael Bishop—and let him spend extra time in the weight room. It would be like going through an off-season conditioning program in-season. We wanted him to work on getting bigger and stronger, but he still had to go to all of the classes and take all of the written tests just like everyone else on the team.

Belichick, like Parcells, was big on giving all of the players a written test in the morning the day before each game and having them turn it in that night. I do the same thing at Notre Dame. There's a separate test for each position on offense and defense. The position coaches are responsible for putting them together, giving them, collecting them, grading them, and then going over the results with the players in their respective groups. For the quarterbacks, you might ask: "Describe the opponent's defensive personnel. . . . Talk about the strengths and weaknesses of each member of the opposing defense. . . . Talk about all of the defensive fronts you expect to see. . . . Talk about the blitzes that the opponent does from a certain front." For the receivers, you might say: "Here are ten formations and plays. Write up what everyone does on each of them."

When you get to within twenty-four hours of kickoff, the game is mental. Your job, as a coach, is done. The tests allow you to see where the players are as they get ready to go into the game. It's basically a review of the scouting report and the game plan, and everything you're doing. Generally, the players I've been around do well on their tests. If they do poorly that allows you to identify the problems and fix them. Or you find out that a player isn't prepared, and he either won't play or will get very little playing time.

One of the things that immediately stood out about Tommy was the great job he did leading all of the other young guys on offense. He would take it upon himself to throw to the younger receivers on his own in practice. Those guys were always around the kid. He had that special something where people just wanted to be around him. I think that's a particularly important quality for a quarterback.

You also could see his natural grasp of the game. In the classroom, with the other quarterbacks, the only other guy that was on the same level intellectually with Drew was Tommy. He would always ask questions during the week, but they would be higher-level questions, astute questions. For instance, if I put on the board a play that had a minor error in the formation, he'd catch it. He would pick those things up as well as the veterans did.

Tommy's only action during our 5–11 season came in the fourth quarter of one game, a blowout loss at Detroit. He threw three passes, completing one. The best thing Tommy did that season was go from something like 185 pounds to 215 pounds. That would make him stronger and more durable.

IN HIS SECOND season, we saw that Tommy could become a starter. Bill and I had a conversation in Tommy's second training camp about putting him ahead of Damon Huard as the number two quarterback, which we did. That decision was a bit controversial because we had just signed Damon, a veteran who had been with the Dolphins, to a two-year contract and given him a million-dollar signing bonus. Tommy didn't see himself at a disadvantage because of his draft status or because he had barely played as a rookie. He went into that camp fully expecting to come out of it number two behind Bledsoe. He was actually trying to be number one, but one step at a time.

It wasn't a landslide where Tommy was much better than Huard on the field. Damon had a good training camp too. We felt that if it was close to even on the field, all of the strengths that Tommy had off the field would move him ahead of the other guy. It was those off-the-field qualities that pushed him ahead.

A major setback for all of us that summer came when Dick Rehbein died suddenly on August 5, 2001, at age forty-five. A pacemaker in his heart stopped. He had passed out on a Saturday while working out at the gym and was rushed to a local hospital. He was later transferred to Massachusetts General Hospital, where he was going to have a stress test on Monday. I talked with him Sunday night. He said, "Well, they're going to give me this test in the morning. I'll try to be back by noon."

I was actually sitting around waiting for him to get back to the office on Monday when some kid who was working as an intern for the team came to the office and told me that Dick had died.

Dick's death affected everybody, me in particular. This was my closest friend on the staff, my right-hand man, my confidant within the team.

After that, Bill got together with me and decided that instead of hiring a new quarterbacks coach, we'd split those duties between us. If we brought someone in so close to the start of the season, he would spend more time just learning rather than working with the quarterbacks, which was what we needed him to do. The approach we took was particularly helpful to a young guy like Tommy because rather than receiving information through an intermediary, he was hearing it directly from me.

In the second week of the season we were playing the Jets, when, late in the game, Drew Bledsoe scrambled to his right. Suddenly, Mo Lewis came flying in from the opposite side and delivered a massive hit on Bledsoe. The first thing I was worried about was Drew's health because he got crushed on that sideline. He returned for a couple of plays after that, then came back out. I remember Damon saying, "He doesn't look right."

We were down by only seven when Tommy entered the game. I wasn't worried about whether he was ready to play. That was who was going in next, right? That was the way we thought as a team. We never worried about whether a guy was ready. Whoever was next, that was who was next. His job was to be ready.

It was tense after the game in the trainers' room. The hit on Bledsoe was so hard that it sheared a blood vessel in his chest. His chest cavity started filling with blood, and he was taken to the hospital. Anytime you have internal bleeding, there are potential problems, and he was having some. We're talking life and death. Thankfully, we got that fixed, but he was going to be out for a while. Although we ended up losing to the Jets, we were confident that Tommy could run the offense well for as long as we needed him in there.

When Drew was eventually healthy, he wanted to go back to being the starter. You never want to lose your starting job as the result of an injury, but in this case it wasn't as simple as just re-storing his previous status. The chemistry and the makeup of the team had changed. When Drew was in there, everyone else was waiting for him to make the play. He was the security blanket. He was always going to be able to bail the team out. As a result, Drew always had a lot of added pressure on him.

When Tommy was in there, the other players knew they had to step up and give him help rather than wait for him to do something. We asked the other players on offense to accept a lot more responsibility, which they did. Our game plans, at least initially, were set up to not make Tommy have to be *the* guy. There would be games when he had to be the guy, but initially—such as in the first game he started, against Indianapolis—we threw a lot of screen passes and little dump-offs. We had good production, but we weren't having him sling it down the field a hundred times to get started. Tommy and the whole team responded well, and we beat the Colts, 44–13.

When you have an expansive offensive package, as we did, you can set up a game plan around what your quarterback can do, just as long as you know what you're dealing with. What's harder is if you lose your quarterback to an injury during a game. It's much more difficult to adjust midstream.

It wasn't all perfect in the beginning. After we beat Indianapolis, we went to Miami and got the crap kicked out of us, 30–10.

A big turning point in Tommy's early development came in our fifth game of the season, against San Diego. We were 1–3 and the Chargers were 3–1. Down by ten points in the fourth quarter, Tommy led us on two scoring drives to tie the game at 26–26, which was how it stood at the end of regulation. Our defense came up with a big stop on the first possession of overtime. Now, the Chargers had one blitz that we had worked on all week long in our meetings and practice. We didn't have many audibles with Tommy in there, but if the Chargers were going to show this one blitz, we were going to audible and have him throw the ball downfield to David Patten on an out-go pattern.

Through sixty minutes, including the fourth quarter, when Tommy was leading us back from a ten-point deficit, San Diego never showed that blitz. On the first play of overtime, sure enough, there it was. The kid saw it, called the audible, and threw about fifty yards downfield to Patten. The Chargers were called for defensive pass interference, putting the ball at the San Diego 40. Six plays later Adam Vinatieri kicked a forty-four-yard field goal to win the game, 29–26.

The fact that Tommy could go through an entire ball game, not see that blitz, go into overtime, see it, and have the presence of mind to make the correct adjustment was phenomenal. Learning it and then actually performing it under duress are two different things.

Everyone used to say that Tommy couldn't throw the ball down the field. That's because in the beginning, we hardly ever threw it deep. It wasn't a question of whether he had the physical ability to make those throws. He has shown he can with the best of them. As Tommy got better and more mature, we gave him more to do—both physically, as far as the play calls, and mentally, allowing him greater latitude at the line of scrimmage. We gave him more and more responsibility.

As the season went on, Tommy got better and better. We weren't lighting it up on offense. We were playing good defense and scoring enough points to win. Through it all, though, we kept seeing progress from Tommy. We won our last six games of the season to finish 11–5 and capture the AFC East Championship. Tommy was 11–3 as a starter. Now he was going to get his first taste of the NFL postseason.

OUR OFFENSE WASN'T at its best in our divisional-round playoff game against the Oakland Raiders—a game that will forever be known as the "Snow Bowl." It was snowing hard and steadily for our final appearance in old Foxboro Stadium, which would give way to the new Gillette Stadium in 2002.

In the fourth quarter, though, it looked like we would be making our final appearance of the season anywhere. We were down, 13–3, and had already gone to our two-minute drill. We did cut the Raiders' lead to 13–10, but they had a chance to put the game away with a little more than two minutes left. All they had to do was pick up a first down on third-and-one from their own 44. Bryan Cox, our veteran linebacker, stuffed Zack Crockett for no gain, they punted, and we got the ball back.

With no time-outs we drove to the Oakland 42. As Tommy dropped back to pass, Charles Woodson came in on a blitz and knocked the ball out of his hand. Greg Biekert recovered near midfield. The officials signaled that it was the Raiders' ball, which also would have meant game over. Even though the replay official upstairs challenged the ruling on the field, Tommy was convinced our season had just ended. He walked off the field looking as dejected as could be. As he got to the sidelines, I told him, "We're going to get the ball back. They're going to call this an incomplete pass."

Tommy looked at me as if I were on drugs, because to him it was not an incomplete pass. To him it was a fumble. Whether I actually knew the call would be reversed after the replay review was irrelevant. It was our only chance of winning the game, so I had to say that, but Tommy wasn't buying it.

After going under the hood to look at the replay monitor for what seemed like an eternity, the referee emerged with the good news: Tommy's arm had been going forward to tuck the ball in, and by rule, Woodson knocking it out of his hand made it an incompletion rather than a fumble. The "Tuck Rule" had kept our season alive, but we would still need another miracle. Adam Vinatieri provided it when he kicked a line-drive forty-five-yard field goal, from about five inches of snow, against the wind, to tie the game at 13–13 and force overtime. That was probably the greatest kick in NFL history, more phenomenal than any of the game winners he has had . . . including his twenty-three-yard field goal in overtime to decide the game.

Even though it was snowing pretty hard, I had thought we would do a lot better offensively than we did. We did have a couple of good "mudders," guys who could always perform well when the field was crummy. One was our tight end, Jermaine Wiggins, who had a game-high ten catches for 68 yards. The other was one of our receivers, David Patten, who finished with eight catches for 107 yards. Of course, we had the Tuck Rule on our side. We felt very fortunate when Tommy's fumble was reversed. Based on the rules, I thought it was the right call. I thought we were lucky, but I also thought it was the right call.

From the beginning of that season I always felt Dick Rehbein's presence. I know that sounds crazy, but I sensed it. The Snow Bowl was no exception. When the Tuck Rule play occurred, the clock initially stopped at 1:43 before the referee reset it to correspond with the incompletion. I didn't realize it at the time, but I found out later that 1:43 is a code that people use on a computer to say "I love you," with each number representing the number of letters in each of the words. Afterward, Rehbein's daughters told me that that was how their father would always end his computer messages to them.

It was almost as if Dick were telling us, "I'm with you, fellas. I've got it covered."

AFTER ALL OF the good fortune we had against Oakland, I wondered if there could be any left for our AFC Championship

Game at Pittsburgh. I was afraid I had gotten my answer late in the first half when running back J. R. Redmond missed a pickup on a safety blitz, and Tommy got hit in the knee. I thought his knee was really messed up. It turned out it wasn't, even though he would not return to the game.

Drew was a little rusty, but he was ready. When he entered the game, we went right down and scored on his eleven-yard touchdown pass to Patten to give us a 14–3 lead. Our defense played great, forcing four turnovers. Our special teams also came up big, with Troy Brown returning a punt fifty-five yards for a touchdown and with a blocked field goal that was also returned for a touchdown.

Once again we weren't stellar on offense. We did just enough to help us win, 24–17, and advance to Super Bowl XXXVI at the Louisiana Superdome, where we would face the St. Louis Rams.

Drew made no attempt to hide the fact that, regardless of Tommy's health, he thought he should be the starter for the Super Bowl. Bill sat down with me, and we both agreed a hundred percent that Tommy would be the starter. We would always agree a hundred percent on a decision like that. Even though Bill was the major decision maker, it would never be a case where Bill said one thing and I said another. We then called Tommy and Drew together to tell them that Tommy was going to start.

Drew wasn't a big fan of that, but we felt that Tommy had gotten us there, and as long as he could practice the Wednesday, Thursday, and Friday before the Super Bowl—which he did—he should get the chance to finish the journey in the driver's seat. That was the one time Drew was mad at me, and at a lot of other people. I could understand why he would be mad. He wanted to be the guy.

That doesn't mean the decision to stay with Tommy was the

wrong one. It was the right one. I'm not saying we were great on offense in 2001, but with Tommy at quarterback we had team chemistry going for us. We had won eight games in a row, including two playoff games, and he had started all of them.

I was a big fan of Drew, whom we would trade to the Bills after the season. He was as tough a quarterback as you could find. As a matter of fact, his toughness sometimes became a weakness because rather than getting rid of the ball, he'd hold it, willing to take the hit to try to make a play. Sometimes that would result in a sack or, worse, a turnover.

I never thought that letting Tommy take us the whole way through the postseason was risky. He was ready. Tommy wasn't a young quarterback anymore. He had been starting since the third game of the year. He practically had a whole season under his belt.

That didn't change the fact that, to the outside world, Tommy was still a "first-year starter." Because of that perception, the Rams' "Greatest Show on Turf" offense, and the fact that they had won the Super Bowl a couple of years earlier, we were considered heavy underdogs, but that wasn't how our team felt. We thought we were going to win. I can't tell you the specific reason for it. It's just something that we all believed as a team.

We still made sure to keep our confidence to ourselves. We loved playing up that underdog role as much as possible. We always played the *no-one-believes-we-can-win* and *it's-us-against-the-world* cards for everything they were worth.

I SPENT MOST of Super Bowl morning watching highlights of previous Super Bowls on the television in my hotel room. After that, I headed downstairs for my last meeting before the game with the entire offense. As I was talking, the lights in the meeting room suddenly went off and right back on again. No one was near the light switch to even bump into it by accident. So either the hotel had a two-second power outage . . . or there was some kind of message being sent.

"Quit screwing with us, Rehbein," I said. No one else in the room laughed or said anything. Either they thought that I had completely lost it, or they shared my belief that Dick was somewhere in our midst.

After the general offensive meeting I met with the quarterbacks. I started talking with Tommy about a couple of the comeback games on those Super Bowl highlights I'd watched in my room.

"Yeah, I was watching those too," he said. "Wouldn't it be cool if it came down to something like that?"

I wasn't nervous. I'm never nervous the day of a game, because I feel prepared. Before the game, I walked over to the section of the wall around the field near where my wife and son were sitting. I told my wife, "After we win this game, you meet me right here because I'll be coming to take you and Charlie down on the field for the celebration." All of the fans who were around them looked at me as if I were on drugs.

Tommy wasn't nervous either. I thought he was ready to go. I verified as much when, on our first offensive play after a Rams punt started us at our 3-yard line, I called, "Zero Flood Slot Hat Seventy-Eight Shout Tosser." We came out with one back, two tight ends, and two wide receivers. We motioned to an empty backfield, and Tommy threw the ball to Troy Brown for a twenty-one-yard gain, seventeen of it after the catch. The drive would end with a punt, but coming out with an aggressive call like that, how much fear could we have had about Tommy being in there? None.

Our defense played great, as Ty Law demonstrated when he intercepted a Kurt Warner pass and returned it forty-seven yards for a touchdown to give us a 7–3 lead in the middle of the second quarter. The success of the Rams' passing game was predicated on the timing between Warner and his receivers, and we were jamming the heck out of their wide receivers to disrupt that timing.

Just before halftime Tommy led us to another touchdown, which came on an eight-yard throw to Patten, to put us up, 14–3. Warner threw another interception, this time to Otis Smith, to set up a Vinatieri field goal that gave us a 17–3 lead at the end of the third quarter.

Of course, you aren't going to stop a quarterback like Warner forever. He led the Rams to two touchdowns in the fourth quarter. All of a sudden the game was tied at 17–17 with 1:30 left in regulation. After the kickoff we got the ball at our own 17. There was 1:21 remaining and we had no time-outs.

Bill turned to me and asked, "What do you think?"

"I think they've got all the momentum," I said. "I think we should go down and try to score."

"Okay, call something safe. If we get a first down here, we'll go ahead and be more aggressive. Let's make sure we don't start off with a sack."

On the first play, Patten was running a go pattern, and if the Rams were in man-to-man coverage, we were laying it up there to him on the left-hand side. They were in zone, however, so Tommy dumped the ball off to Redmond on a check down for a five-yard gain. It looked as if Belichick's fears about us starting off with a sack might come true, as Tommy actually got touched by Leonard Little, but he stepped up to make the throw. On the second play Tommy threw another check down to Redmond for eight yards to our 30-yard line.

After a spike to stop the clock at forty-one seconds, Tommy threw a flare-control pass—which is when you dump the ball off to a back or a tight end when downfield receivers are covered—to the left to Redmond, who made a defender miss and picked up eleven yards before getting pushed out of bounds at our 41 to stop the clock with thirty-three seconds left. If Redmond hadn't gone out of bounds, we would probably have had Tommy kneel down and just take it to overtime. Once Redmond made it to the 41 and the clock stopped, we went from make-sure-they-don't-get-the-ball-back-and-score mode to try-to-win-it mode. Now we were being more aggressive.

We then called the same play twice in a row with different personnel groupings. The first was a pass to Jermaine Wiggins, who was running an in-cut. The Rams brought a weak-safety blitz, which would normally have triggered a sight adjustment, where the quarterback throws to a wide receiver on a slant route to the left-hand side. However, Tommy knew that if we threw the slant to the left-hand side, the clock might run out, so instead he rolled to the right and threw the ball away, stopping the clock at twenty-nine seconds.

We changed personnel on the next play, replacing the tight end with a fourth wide receiver. We called the exact same play, but now the guy running the in-cut was Troy Brown rather than Wiggins. This time, instead of blitzing, as they'd done on the previous play, the Rams played "Two Tampa," which is where both safeties are positioned deep to prevent the deep pass (the name comes from the Tampa Bay Buccaneers, who made the coverage popular when Tony Dungy was their coach), and a middle linebacker drops to the middle of the field.

Tommy was reading "high-low" off the middle linebacker, London Fletcher, meaning that if Fletcher played "high" and covered the deep receiver, Tommy would throw to the underneath receiver, and if Fletcher played "low" and covered the underneath receiver, Tommy would throw to the deep receiver. Fletcher played "high," and Tommy threw underneath for fourteen yards to Troy, who picked up nine more yards after the catch before going out of bounds at the St. Louis 36 to stop the clock with twenty-one seconds remaining. I put Wiggins back in and called "Sixty-eight Return."

"Just dump the ball to Wiggins," I told Tommy on the coach-to-quarterback communication system. "Let's get ourselves some extra yards and let Adam come in and win this game. And make sure everyone knows that we're going to come back and clock the ball after the completion."

Tommy called the play and threw the ball to Wiggins for a six-yard gain; then everyone lined up so that he could spike the ball and stop the clock, which he did with seven seconds left. Adam came on and kicked a forty-eight-yard field goal as time expired. Final score: Patriots 20, Rams 17. MVP: Tom Brady.

When everyone ran on that field, I did exactly what I had promised to do before the game and went right to the stands to get Maura and Charlie so that they could be part of the celebration. This Super Bowl win felt different from the first one with the Giants because back then I was only a research guy. It felt different from the one the Patriots lost in New Orleans in 1996, when I was their receivers coach. Now, I had something to do with whether we won or lost. I was going to have a legacy one way or another. For all of us on that team, this would be a legacy for the ages.

Other than the Jets beating the Colts in Super Bowl III, it was probably the biggest upset ever. To say we were joyous after that game would be an understatement. Delirious was more like it.

9

Weighty Issues

I would never have survived my gastric bypass nightmare without my best friend and love of my life, Maura. *(Courtesy of the author)*

"There's a saying that it usually happens to the good ones."

—Doctor at Massachusetts General Hospital
to Maura Weis

Not long after Super Bowl XXXVI, I was watching a DVD of the game. I said, "Look at that fat ass!" I wish I had been looking at someone else. Unfortunately, that fat ass was me.

I had always been a pudge-ball, but seeing how I looked on the sidelines of that game motivated me to take drastic measures. I had been on a yo-yo diet for about fifteen years, where I would yo-yo over and under three hundred pounds. At that point, I was well over three hundred pounds. I felt that I was headed toward a heart attack, and that I owed it to my family to do something that would help me to stay alive as long as I could.

I thought the best solution was gastric bypass surgery.

I had seen the success stories. Al Roker, the weatherman for NBC's *Today* show, had become the poster child for the procedure.

I figured, If it worked for him, it could work for me. I started to do some research, but not as much as I should have. About two weeks after I started to look into having the surgery, I was talking with a doctor about actually doing it. About a month later, on Friday, June 14, 2002, I was on an operating table at Massachusetts General Hospital.

I was told that I would have a one-night stay in the hospital and that I would be sent home at some point in the afternoon of Saturday, June 15. We were planning to leave on vacation for the Jersey Shore three days later. Within five days of the surgery, you're supposed to be getting around well.

Maura and my son were both mad at me for deciding to have the surgery. They absolutely didn't want me to do it. I wasn't fearful going into it, but I did tell my wife, "Watch me be the one where something goes wrong."

I wanted to keep the whole thing as private as possible. I told very few people I was having the surgery and checked into the hospital under a false name. When the procedure was finished, I was wheeled out of the operating room to another place upstairs. I was complaining about stomach pains, but it didn't cause any alarm. Figuring everything had gone well and there was nothing to do but let me sleep, Maura went home with the intention of picking me up the next day.

Late that night my stomach, which had been leaking, burst. I had to be rushed back to the intensive-care unit. I was bleeding internally, which caused me to have severe respiratory difficulties. At about six o'clock on Saturday morning, somebody from the hospital called Maura at home and said, "You'd better come in here. We've got a problem." Maura had our cleaning lady come over to watch our kids. When Maura got to the hospital, I was in bad shape. I started undergoing multiple blood transfusions.

On Sunday, the doctors gave me a test that showed that I had massive internal bleeding. They determined that I would need emergency surgery to stop the bleeding.

"What choice do I have?" I asked them.

"None," they said. "You'll die if you don't have the operation."

Apparently, I was coherent enough to sign the consent forms. I say apparently because I don't remember signing them, and my wife would not sign them. She was afraid that I would die on the table.

I had the surgery. The internal bleeding had led to sepsis, or infection, and I lapsed into a coma after the operation. It was bad, really bad. It was bad enough that at one point it looked like I was going to die. I was even administered last rites by a Catholic priest while connected to a ventilator in the intensive-care unit.

Tommy Brady, who was one of the few people aware that I was having the gastric bypass surgery, had stopped by the hospital on Saturday morning to see how I was doing. He just showed up so he wouldn't have to listen to me nag him for not stopping to see me. He never bargained for what he would find when he got there.

Basically, it was Tommy's support that got Maura through Saturday and Sunday until the reinforcements—our out-of-town family and other friends—could get there on Monday. If it hadn't been for him, Maura would have gone off the deep end.

I don't remember very much, because I was in a coma for most of this time. I do remember that in my brief moments of

consciousness, I was fighting for my family. I just remember saying, "I can't die. . . . I can't die." Maura and Tommy also told me
that I said, "They're trying to take me, but I won't let them." I don't
know what that means, but Maura and Tommy told me I said
that.

On Tuesday, while I was still in intensive care and connected
to a ventilator, one of the doctors told Maura for the first time that
it didn't look like I was going to make it.

"He's a good man," Maura told her.

"There's a saying that it usually happens to the good ones," the
doctor said.

That was the first time that Maura actually believed that I
might die.

MORE THAN A week later, I came out of the coma and was
moved upstairs to a private room. I still had a long way to go before I was out of the woods. I still had blood clots that at any moment could go right to my heart, and that would be it.

Maura wasn't telling Charlie, who was nine at the time, how
bad I was. It was a while before she even brought him to the hospital. I remember him coming to see me with my nephew. It was
pretty scary for both of them, but Charlie's a trooper.

Every night at Mass General, I was afraid to go to sleep, because I thought it would be my last night. The only time I felt safe
was when Maura was there. As soon as she would arrive, I would
fall asleep. When I woke up, she'd tell me she was going to leave,
and I'd say, "But you just got here." In reality, she had been there
for twelve hours, but I'd slept so soundly, I'd think she had been
there for only ten minutes.

While attending Patriots games, Maura had met Dr. Joe Amaral, who is the president and CEO of Rhode Island Hospital in Providence. On July 5, exactly three weeks after the surgery, she brought him up to visit me at Mass General. When Maura left the room to get a cup of coffee, I said, "Joe, get me the hell out of here. Whatever you do, do not leave here without transferring me out of this hospital and into Rhode Island Hospital."

After a little more discussion, he actually got me a bed at Rhode Island Hospital and called an ambulance. Hours later, I was on my way. I spent a week at Rhode Island Hospital. After that, I spent a week at a rehab hospital affiliated with Rhode Island Hospital before I was sent home in a wheelchair.

I developed severe nerve damage in my legs. As a result, I have permanently lost some feeling in both of my feet. Before the gastric bypass surgery, I had no problem walking, jogging, or playing sports. All of those things went by the boards after the surgery.

The doctors told me the condition was temporary and that after two or three months I'd be able to walk without restrictions. Four years later, nothing has changed. The feeling I have in my left foot is about 80 percent of normal, while the right one is about 50 percent of normal. That's as good as both feet will ever get. If I closed my eyes and you touched the bottom of my right foot, I wouldn't know you were touching it.

When I first got home from the rehab hospital, I couldn't even walk. Maura made our home wheelchair accessible, installing a ramp so that I could get into the house and creating extra room to allow me to get in and out of the bathroom. She also turned our library on the main level into a bedroom for me because I couldn't walk steps.

After three days, I told Maura, "Get rid of that wheelchair."
I started using a walker. I didn't move very fast. I was taking
it, literally, about an inch at a time. I'd go an inch . . . then another inch . . . then another inch. The more strength I gained,
the farther I was able to move, although at first it wasn't very far.
I had big plastic braces to help support my legs. We hired people
from the rehab hospital to come to the house each morning to
take me through physical therapy. They were great. Trainers
from the Patriots also came to the house to help me with my
rehab.

Going through a near-death experience causes you to do a lot
of reflecting. It gave me an opportunity to go back and think
about things that had happened over the last decade that, in hind-
sight, I would do differently if I had the chance. It also gave me an
opportunity to appreciate the people who have figured signifi-
cantly in my life.

Not long after the surgery, I wrote Bill Parcells a letter in
which I told him, "Look, you're the reason why I'm in this league.
For me not to be respectful or thankful or appreciative of that fact
is wrong. I want you to know that I realize any success I have in
this league, ultimately, comes back to you giving me a chance
back in 1990."

While I was on the mend, I also had some mending to do with
my own family. My wife and son cared for me and helped me to
get better, but once I was strong enough to handle it they let me
know, in no uncertain terms, that I wasn't very smart. I've called
myself a "dumb ass" many days for having the gastric bypass procedure. It was probably the biggest mistake of my life.

Tommy Brady was the one person who was there with my

wife through that whole ordeal. During rookie camp, which rookies and all of the quarterbacks attend for about a week before the full squad arrives for the start of regular training camp, he would finish up with the quarterback meetings at night and then drive over to my house just to perk me up. My wife would say to me that the only part of the day when I tried to gather myself up to not act like I was sick was when he came over. Tommy would just sit and talk with me for about an hour before going back to camp in time for bed check. We'd talk football, but we'd talk about everything else, too. Somewhere, in every conversation, Tommy would say, "You've got to get back." He was really pushing me.

It wasn't just that he took the time to come over to see me. He genuinely cared. I feel forever indebted to Tommy. Now, I never changed my approach to coaching him. In fact, at one point when they were in the hospital, Tommy said to Maura, "Do you think that this will mean that he won't yell at me as much?" Simultaneously, they shook their heads, laughed, and said, "Nah, that's not going to happen."

There would still be many times when Tommy's opinion didn't count with me, just like any other player's, but our relationship definitely changed. It was like family now. He became like a son to me. You'll never, ever hear me say a bad thing about Tommy Brady as a person for as long as I live.

Damon Huard and Rohan Davey, our backup quarterbacks, also showed a great deal of concern. Damon was at the hospital when things went bad. Maura said he almost vomited right in my room. That was how awful everything looked at that point. Tommy got queasy too.

- - -

AS THE TEAM got ready for training camp, the jury was still out as to what was going to happen to me. Given the condition I was in, Bill Belichick could have gone out and hired my replacement, and I don't think anyone would have blamed him if he had. To his credit, he waited for me to recover.

The weekend that regular training camp opened at Bryant College at Smithfield, Rhode Island, I called Joe Amaral and asked if he would come to my house the next day and then drive me over to camp so that I could say hello to the coaches and everyone else there. I had my walker because I still wasn't able to get around without it. As soon as we got there, people acted as if they'd seen a ghost because I looked so bad.

Starting the following Monday, a young guy from the Patriots would come to my house to pick me up and drive me to camp. I'd work for about three or four hours each day and then go home. I got around with a motorized cart. Later in camp, when I took over calling the offensive plays, I would get out of the cart and use a four-pronged cane. I had plastic braces, from my foot to my knee, on both legs.

I used that cart the whole year, even inside the office. I felt no embarrassment about doing that. If I'd felt embarrassment, I'd never have gotten on that cart and gone out on the practice field and coached. I sucked it up and went out there because I felt that that was what I was supposed to do.

In the very beginning maybe the other coaches and members of the Patriots' front office treated me a little differently. Before the first preseason game against the Giants in the Meadowlands,

Belichick said, "I don't think, with where you are physically, that you should go."

Granted, I was not in very good shape, but I still wanted to make the trip.

"What do you mean?" I said. "I've been back here for over a week."

"Charlie, until you can start working close to a normal day, it wouldn't be good for you to do this," Bill said.

The team went to the Meadowlands to play the Giants, and I stayed behind. The next day I was at work for twelve hours. My wife was really pissed at me now.

I was hurting. The pain started in my feet, but I could feel it just about everywhere. I was revved up on pain pills, mainly Tylenol with codeine. I stopped taking everything before the season because I didn't feel my mind was sharp enough when I was using that stuff. The only exception was Coumadin, a blood thinner, so I wouldn't get any blood clots.

I spent one preseason game in the coaches' booth. I think Bill wanted me up there because he was looking out for my safety. I was on the sidelines for the rest of the games that year.

Once the season began I worked full days. It wasn't easy being on my feet for long stretches. For twenty-four hours after a game, I would be wincing with pain, which would ease as the week went on. Then it would start all over again the next game.

I had told Damon Huard and Rohan Davey that their number one job was to make sure that they protected me on the sidelines. One stood on my left and one stood on my right. They looked out for me, although I still ended up getting knocked over once that year, when we played the Jets at the Meadowlands.

When you don't have any mobility, some accidents are unavoidable.

I didn't talk to any media about what I went through, which was fairly easy because Bill had a policy that no assistant coaches could talk with the media. *Good Morning America* wanted to talk with me about gastric bypass from a negative perspective, which would have been opposite of the view presented by its direct competitor, the *Today* show, because of Al Roker. *People* magazine wanted to talk with me too. I said no to both of them.

One interview I did do was with Chris Mortensen for ESPN.com. Afterward, he wrote that the pursuit of a head-coaching job was the number one reason that I had the gastric bypass surgery. It wasn't. I'll not deny that it could have affected me not getting a head-coaching job at that point. It was part of the story, but it was not the number one reason.

The number one reason was my family. The reality was that I had the surgery because my father died at fifty-six. I had the surgery because I have a special-needs daughter. I had the surgery because I have a son. I had the surgery because I have a young wife. I felt I owed it to them to do everything I could to reduce my chances of dying at an early age.

Now, did the gastric bypass work to the extent that I lost weight? Yes. Once I recovered, I was on a diet that a person who has had gastric bypass would follow, which meant I ate hardly anything. Your stomach starts out the size of an egg, but then it grows. But I still can't eat anywhere near what I used to eat.

I initially lost about a hundred pounds. I gained about thirty of it back and have stayed pretty consistent with my weight since. I'm not as heavy as I was before the surgery, but I paid far too heavy a price. Any possible benefit I may have gotten from the surgery is not worth being at death's door, or having only 50 percent movement in my right foot and 80 percent movement in my left foot.

After all of my complications became public, several people from around the country who were considering gastric bypass surgery called or wrote me to ask my advice. I would call back every one of these people and privately discuss the surgery. I never tried to talk anyone out of it. I just shared my own feelings based on my own experience.

"You do what you want," I'd say. "I would never do it again in a million years."

We went 9–7 that season and missed the playoffs. We were inconsistent that year on offense. Not to be a martyr, but I believed that my condition cost us at least one game. I don't know which game it was, but the difference between 10–6 and 9–7 was the difference between making the playoffs and missing the playoffs and a possible Super Bowl. I hold myself accountable for us losing a seventh game and not winning a tenth one.

I didn't do anything that I didn't normally do, I promise you. I can't remember one game where I thought that I alone screwed it up, but because the season turned out as it did, I put the blame on myself. That's how I think. I'm sure I wasn't alone. I'm sure there were others who felt the same way.

IN HIS FOURTH season, 2003, Tommy had much more command of the team. He had a very calm demeanor. He wasn't just the fired-up young guy that he had been when he first started. Everyone on the team had confidence that he could win the game for us.

In our first Super Bowl win, our defense played great and we did enough on offense to win. Now, offensively, we felt that we could do enough to hold up our end of the bargain. If the game had to be one of those games where the offense played exceptionally well, we were capable of doing that. After a 2–2 start, that ability played a big part in helping us to go 12–0 through the rest of the regular season.

By this point, the empty-backfield formation with five wide receivers was a staple of our offense. The dilemma that it poses to a defense is that you have to cover all five guys who are running pass patterns, which leaves you with only six defenders to do something else. What are you going to do with them?

Are you going to bring six to rush the passer? Are you going to bring five? Are you going to bring four? Are you going to bring three? If you do bring all six, you had better get to him, because he has five receivers in one-on-one coverage, and somewhere out there is a mismatch that he can exploit.

Ron Erhardt was the biggest influence on my use of the empty backfield after he got it going with the Pittsburgh Steelers in the early nineties. It wasn't like I was reinventing the wheel. Ron had success with it long before I ever started using it. I just made some of my own modifications. For instance, when Ron went to empty, he would usually use one personnel group consisting of multiple wide receivers, whereas we did it from multiple personnel groups, one of which included two backs, two receivers, and one tight end. That way we could get favorable pass-coverage matchups against a regular defense, which is better equipped to stop the run than the pass, as opposed to a dime defense, which has more cover guys on the field.

Based on the personnel group you have out there, the defense doesn't know whether or not you're going to go empty. You could be using an I formation for all the defense knows. Now when you go empty and spread the defense with five guys who can catch the ball, you can end up with linebackers in pass coverage—and some mismatches.

To be successful with the empty-backfield formation, you need a quarterback who can recognize the weakness of the coverage and direct the protection to pick up the most dangerous pass rushers, and you must have guys that can get open. The hardest part for the quarterback is figuring out how many guys are going to rush him.

Tommy Brady has become the best at doing that by far. I don't think anyone's a close second. I know Neil O'Donnell had good success with the formation in Pittsburgh, and he did some of it when we were with the Jets, but Brady took it to another level.

Sometimes, whether you're in empty or any other formation, you get into a great groove when you're calling plays. You feel like it's all going to work. That isn't always the case, of course, but you do have those times when you know you can do no wrong with your play selection.

There are also those occasions when everyone else watching the game says, "Why the hell are they calling that play?" Rest assured we're doing it for a reason. There are always reasons you do certain things in a game, and when you call a play that doesn't seem to make any sense for a particular situation, you do it because you're trying to set up another play. As soon as you call one play you're already betting the odds of what could happen off of that play so you can get your choices ready for the next play.

One of the biggest problems play callers have is they're not thinking of the next play. They're watching the play they just called and waiting for the result before they decide what they're going to do next. When I call a play, you'll always see me looking right down to the call sheet for the next play even while the play I just called is being delivered in the huddle.

If I call a pass, I already know the play I'm going to call if it's complete and the play I'm going to call if it's incomplete. Often, when you see a team penalized for delay of game or when it looks like guys don't know what they're doing, that's because the play caller has not thought through what might happen on the play previously called and what his alternatives are going to be based on that play.

It's not hard to avoid getting so caught up in the game that you don't stay one play ahead, because staying one play ahead is what you're supposed to do. I also figured out early on that the best way to take advantage of the coach-to-quarterback communication system is to give the quarterback some coaching points after you give him the play. You can't do that if you're not giving him the play fast enough, because the system automatically turns off at the fifteen-second mark of the forty-second play clock.

You want to be able to deliver your information fast enough so that he can call the play in the huddle and get out of the huddle, and you can still say a couple of things to him before the system cuts off. Maybe a little reminder such as "We're in the red zone, don't take a sack. . . . Take a peek at the X receiver before you go to the strong side."

As Tommy became more mature, getting the information to him as quickly as possible also gave him time to go to the line of scrimmage and say, "Well, this play's better than that play. Let's get out of this one. Let's go with that one."

You always script the first fifteen or twenty plays. Why? Obviously, one of the reasons is to try to score. The players have already practiced the plays that you're going to call. Another reason you do it is to see how the defense is going to play against the different personnel groups or the different formations you put out there.

From one formation you'll have multiple plays. Some plays will be better than others against what the defense is doing. You usually get through the whole script, but sometimes I've thrown out the script after only nine plays because what we were doing wasn't working.

You've got to be willing to change. It's one thing when you have that script of fifteen to twenty plays and you're just calling them in order. Once you're past that stage, you're calling plays based on what's happening in the game. That's when you really have to be creative.

Late in Tommy's first year as a starter, we were playing the Jets at the Meadowlands and they were kicking our ass in the first half. We couldn't block them. Tommy had been sacked twice and was getting pressured the entire half, which had the most to do with putting us in a 13–0 hole. I threw out the game plan that had had him taking five- or seven-step drops—which is what you do on longer-developing pass plays—and we went with three-step drops that had him getting rid of the ball quickly. We had no choice, because we couldn't block them long enough for anything but a three-step drop. The adjustment worked. We came back for a 17–16 win.

I'm not afraid to make a mistake. Too many times in life people are afraid to make a mistake and are not very aggressive.

I also bank on fifteen to twenty years of experience and the volumes of stuff that I've done. I'll call something that I haven't called in three years. In our last game of the 2005 regular season at Notre Dame, we ran a play that I hadn't called since the Patriots faced the Carolina Panthers in the Super Bowl.

I never panic. I never feel pressure during a game. Ever. It doesn't make any difference what the magnitude of the game is. It doesn't make any difference whether we're winning or losing. When the people around you see that you're not panicking and that you can handle the pressure, it calms them down.

If you know what you're doing, you don't feel pressure. Pressure is something that's self-inflicted. Different people handle it different ways. The key to not letting it get the better of you is preparation. If you're prepared and know what you're doing, you should be able to handle the pressure because you should feel confident that you have the answers to the test.

Confident, not giddy. You're never giddy. Contrary to popular opinion, I don't actually enjoy this stuff. Everybody thinks you enjoy this stuff. This is a job. This is what you do. When you call the play and it works, that's enjoyable.

Of course, for every play that works, there's a play that doesn't work. You don't harp too much on the ones that work. You harp on the ones that don't work.

THE BEST OPPORTUNITY I had to become a head coach in the NFL was after the '03 season, when the Bills were looking for a replacement for Gregg Williams. I had what I thought was a great interview with Tom Donahoe, the Bills' general manager at the time, on January 1, 2004, at the Westin Hotel in Providence. I also had a great phone conversation with the Bills' owner, Ralph Wilson. Those conversations followed an interview I had had with the Giants, who were searching for a replacement for Dan Reeves.

On January 6 the Giants hired Tom Coughlin, who had been out of coaching for a year after guiding the Jacksonville Jaguars. Four days later, before our divisional-round playoff game against Tennessee at Gillette Stadium, I received a call basically informing me that if we lost the game that night to the Titans, I'd be the new head coach of the Bills. I would have been in Buffalo the next day.

The same person also told me that if we won the game, the Bills might be moving in another direction because they wouldn't be able to offer me the job until the Patriots' season was over. This was all about timing because the Bills wanted to fill the job as soon as they could, and I wasn't the only candidate out there.

I won't reveal who made the call, but I will tell you that it wasn't Donahoe, or anyone else working in management for the Bills. Let's just say it was from a very reliable person who knew what was going on within their team.

Before that game, I went to our owner, Robert Kraft, to let him know that I had gotten that phone call and to pass along that information to the commissioner, Paul Tagliabue, who was going to be at our game. I was concerned that if we lost, it could be perceived that I threw the game to get the head-coaching job. I said that no one would ever have to worry about that with me, but I just wanted it on the record because I didn't want ever to be thought of as someone who would do something like that.

I knew that I'd be better off financially if we lost the game. My wife knew that too, and neither of us was happy knowing that what would be good for us would be bad for the Patriots and doing everything I could to help them win another Super Bowl. Yet, I never felt conflicted or awkward about the situation, because I addressed it right off the bat with the right people.

The temperature was four degrees at kickoff, with a wind chill of minus ten, making it the coldest game in Patriot history. It was the coldest game I can ever remember as a coach, and that includes one in a blinding snowstorm in Buffalo. We threw a touchdown pass early, Brady to Bethel Johnson, for forty-one yards, but we knew we were in for a tough challenge.

The Titans were a good team. They kept lining up in an empty-backfield formation, and Bill Belichick and Romeo Crennel, our defensive coordinator, kept bringing the house. On fourth-and-twelve from the New England 42, Steve McNair laid up a pass that would have put the Titans in field-goal range with under two minutes left, but Drew Bennett dropped it. That allowed us to kill off the final 1:38 to seal a 17–14 victory.

Because I would be unavailable for at least another week as we advanced to the AFC Championship Game, the Bills took me out of consideration for the job. Two days later they hired Mike Mularkey, who had been the offensive coordinator of the Steelers.

Once that opportunity was gone, I didn't worry about it any longer. There was nothing I could do about it. We were getting ready to play the AFC Championship Game against the Colts. We were just trying to win two more games. I didn't have enough time to feel sorry for myself.

Going into the conference-title game, our team game plan—meaning for offense, defense, and special teams—was to control the ball and prevent another shootout like we had had in the regular season in the RCA Dome. We came out on top in that one, 38–34, but only after stopping the Colts four times at our 1-yard line at the end of the game. This time, we had the ball thirty-two minutes and fourteen seconds to the Colts' twenty-seven minutes and forty-six seconds on the way to a 24–14 victory and Super Bowl XXXVIII in Houston.

SUPER BOWL XXXVIII, between the Patriots and the Carolina Panthers, was being hyped as a battle between two head coaches with two great defensive minds. It was the "Bill Belichick vs. John Fox Bowl."

Sure enough, at the end of the first quarter there was no score, and the feeling-out process continued into the second quarter. We were moving the ball but not scoring. They weren't even moving the ball. They were getting the crap kicked out of them. Finally, late in the first half, the teams started trading scores, and all of a sudden we were up 14–10.

At halftime we felt that, offensively, we had them reeling. We thought we had a good idea of what they were doing, and we knew what we wanted to do. We had moved the ball well in the first quarter, but just not gotten any points to show for it.

One of the focal points of our game plan was Ricky Manning, the Panthers' rookie cornerback. Wherever he was, that's where Brady was throwing. Manning had just had three picks against Philadelphia in the NFC Championship Game, and he'd been talking all sorts of trash. We lined David Givens up on him, and it was a massacre. Givens didn't catch every ball thrown his way, but it was a physical mismatch.

After a scoreless third quarter, the game turned into a shootout. With a 21–16 lead midway through the fourth quarter, we had a chance to put it away on third-and-goal from the Carolina 9, but

Tommy threw an interception for the first time in what seemed like forever. The Panthers then took it down for a touchdown to go ahead, 22–21. We came back with a touchdown and a two-point conversion, and they answered with a touchdown. It was 29–29 with a minute and eight seconds left. We found ourselves tied in another Super Bowl with a chance to drive for the winning score.

There were two big differences between this situation and the one Tommy faced in Super Bowl XXXVI. This time, we had three time-outs; back then, we had none. This time, thanks to John Kasay's kickoff going out of bounds, we started on our 40-yard line; back then, we were on our 17.

Tommy threw a pass to Troy Brown to give us a first down at the Carolina 47. He threw another pass to Troy in the left seam, but this time Troy got called for offensive pass interference that pushed us back to our 43. Tommy threw yet another pass to Troy to get us to the Carolina 44 and followed that up with a four-yard throw to Daniel Graham. On third-and-three from the 40, I moved Deion Branch, who would normally be the outside receiver on the left-hand side, into the slot, and I moved Troy, who would normally be in the slot, to the outside receiver spot on the right-hand side, where Givens normally lined up. The idea was to have Branch, who was our fastest receiver, run the deeper route.

I knew John Fox's coaching tendencies going back to his days as the defensive coordinator for the Giants when I was an assistant with the Jets. We played the Giants every year in the preseason, and we also played them once in the 1999 regular season. The only things they were doing in this game were blitzing with five to seven defenders, which John likes to do if he's pressuring, or playing five under/two deep, which means five defenders covering man-to-man underneath and two safeties covering deep.

I guessed that they would play five under/two deep, and they did. Tommy would have two open receivers, one deep and one short. He threw it to Branch for a seventeen-yard gain to the 23-yard line with nine seconds to go.

Out came Adam Vinatieri to settle a second Super Bowl with his foot, this time from forty-one yards. Final score: Patriots 32, Panthers 29. MVP: Tommy Brady.

10

Working a Double Shift While Trying to Avoid Double Trouble

A third Super Bowl win was the perfect way for Bill Belichick, Romeo Crennel, and me to celebrate our last game together. *(Photograph by David Silverman)*

"Here's who I am. Here's what I've got to offer. Are you interested?"

—Charlie Weis, calling a Notre Dame recruit

You didn't have to worry about the Patriots becoming too full of themselves after winning a second Super Bowl in three seasons, because we had learned our lesson by going 9–7 after the first one. I think everyone—every coach, every player—was determined to avoid another letdown. We had experienced how awful it felt. Nobody wanted to feel that again.

We traded for Corey Dillon, a very talented running back who had wanted out of Cincinnati. I was at a Boston Bruins hockey game at the Fleet Center with my son when I got the call on my cell phone that the deal was done. I immediately called Corey to welcome him to the team while sitting behind the Bruins' bench, trying to hear him over the crowd.

I was happy to have him. My first impression when I met Corey was that, at six one and 225 pounds, he was a big man. As

I studied videotape of him playing for the Bengals I saw that he could do everything. He could run inside. He could run outside. He could run with power. He also was fast for a guy of his size. He had already rushed for a zillion yards in his career, so it wasn't like we were going to reinvent Corey Dillon.

For all of the media attention over his unhappiness in Cincinnati, I never had a problem with him. Not once. He was as nice a kid as I've ever had. I think he just wanted to go somewhere and win. He liked play-action and we liked to run play-action. It's always easier to run play-action when you have a running back of his caliber.

Before Dillon's arrival we didn't have a consistently strong running game, but we would still run and still use play-action. One of the biggest mistakes on offense is heavily emphasizing your average yards per carry. I'm much more concerned with having a high volume of running plays because it usually means that you're winning.

We were winning in 2004. We won our first six games of the season to extend our winning streak to twenty-one games, dating back to '03. On October 31 of '04, we faced the Steelers at Heinz Field. Our whole game plan was to pound it inside, then play-action to take advantage of the aggressive nature of the Steelers' defense taking shots downfield.

However, Dillon pulled a hammy in warm-ups before that game, so he was out. Now Kevin Faulk was in at running back, but Kevin was not a pound-it guy, so that pretty much killed our game plan. We ended up losing by fourteen points, but the game wasn't even that close.

We bounced back nicely by going on another six-game winning streak. The sixth win was against Cincinnati, the same weekend I accepted the Notre Dame job. After flying to South Bend for the news conference introducing me as the new coach of the Fighting Irish, I promptly returned to Foxboro to begin preparation for our next game, at Miami, on *Monday Night Football.*

To help make certain that no one in the building talked with me about Notre Dame and that no phone calls pertaining to Notre Dame came directly to me, Belichick assigned Shane Waldron, who was the assistant to the Patriots' football operations guy, to act as my gatekeeper for all Notre Dame–related business. If assistant coaches from the Patriots or anywhere else wanted to talk with me about hiring them or recommending somebody as an assistant coach, they would have to go to Shane. If people from Notre Dame wanted to talk with me on the phone, they would have to call Shane.

Each day around noon I would meet with Shane, who would go on to become an offensive graduate assistant on my Notre Dame staff, and he would give me the rundown of messages. I would make the corresponding phone calls in my free time.

Four days after being introduced as Notre Dame's new coach, I returned to South Bend for twenty-four hours to interview all of the members of the existing coaching staff, none of whom would be retained. Then I flew back to New England and took off with the rest of the team to Miami.

We lost to the Dolphins, 29–28. We moved the ball well, picking up more than three hundred yards in total offense, and that was something we normally didn't do against the Dolphins. However, Tommy threw four interceptions, including just an awful throw at the end of the game. Of course, all of the people in New England were blaming me for us losing to the Dolphins. *Charlie*

Weis is only worried about the Notre Dame job. He's thrown in the towel on the Patriots.

Nothing could have been further from the truth. I was putting every bit as much effort into the Patriots as I was into Notre Dame. I was literally working two full-time jobs for the rest of the season. On my normal schedule for the Patriots, I would work until eleven o'clock at night. After I took the Notre Dame job I would do my work for the Patriots until eight o'clock at night, then make three hours of recruiting calls for Notre Dame. The best time to make recruiting calls is from 8 P.M. to 11 P.M. because that's usually when the kids are home, and under NCAA rules, you're allowed to talk directly to them in December.

After finishing the calls, I would make up the three hours I took away from my offensive coordinator duties by working from 11 P.M. to 2 A.M. on football stuff for the Patriots. I was going on about three hours of sleep, but I could handle it because very often in training camp I was on that same kind of schedule. Bill knew exactly what I was doing and how I was doing it. I went over the plan with him. He trusted me. He trusted that I was going to do what I said I was going to do.

I also explained to Maura and Charlie that I was going to have to go into a training-camp mentality until the season was over, which, we hoped, wouldn't be until after we won another Super Bowl. We were all in this together as a family. Everyone got a vote on whether or not we wanted to take this job, and we were unanimous in voting for it. Everyone also knew what was going to come along with it, including the fact that I would be spending more time away from home than usual.

I worked from a list of names and telephone numbers supplied by the recruiting coordinator who was already at Notre Dame, so these were kids that Ty Willingham and his staff had been pursuing. I would just tell the kids the truth. I'd say, "Look, I can't sit here and tell you about the relationship that you and I have. You had relationships with all of these other people who were here. Here's who I am. Here's what I've got to offer. Are you interested?"

If they said yes, I'd keep talking. If they said no, I'd move on. If they were not interested, I was not going to try to make them interested, and the conversation would be over within five minutes.

It wasn't difficult or awkward to pick up a process that someone else had started. The difficulty was that I did not have a single person on the coaching staff. I was it. I spoke with hundreds of recruits. I figured we were going to lose out on some kids that first year, but win out on many more the following year because of all of the extra publicity that we were going to get from the Patriots' playoff run. As far as I was concerned, the best thing that could happen to Notre Dame football would be the Patriots winning the Super Bowl. I would walk out of New England with my head held high, and at the same time I would get all of that free press for the Fighting Irish.

I hired all of my assistant coaches by phone. I didn't have time to conduct face-to-face interviews. I knew it was a risk to do it all by phone, but that was the only way I could do it. Otherwise, I would have fallen so far behind in recruiting and in all of my other work for 2005 and beyond that it would have been nearly impossible to recover. I met most of the members of the staff for the first time during our bye week right before we went to dinner at a recruiting weekend at Notre Dame. I stuck with my plan of putting together a staff that would have at least two guys on both sides of the ball who had worked together at some point so they would already have some rapport, people whose coaching I was familiar with, alumni of the school, and people with backgrounds as recruiting coordinators.

This is how I addressed those areas: On offense, I hired David Cutcliffe as the quarterbacks coach and John Latina as the offensive line coach because they had worked together when Cutcliffe (who later left because of a heart problem) was head coach at the University of Mississippi and Latina was his offensive line coach and offensive coordinator. On defense, I hired Rick Minter as the defensive coordinator/linebackers coach and Jappy Oliver as the defensive line coach because they had worked together with Lou Holtz at South Carolina. I hired Bill Lewis as assistant head coach on defense/defensive backs and Bernie Parmalee as the tight ends coach from the Dolphins staff. I respected Bill from going against the Dolphins' defense all of the time when I was with the Patriots, and I had actually coached Bernie when he was a running back with the Jets, and was a big fan of his as well. I was more familiar with them than with anyone else I hired.

Both coordinators I hired had a previous connection with Notre Dame. Mike Haywood, our offensive coordinator, was a former Notre Dame cornerback that I hired from the coaching staff at the University of Texas. I knew he was hardened because he had worked for Nick Saban at LSU and for Mack Brown at Texas. Minter had been Lou Holtz's defensive coordinator back in the early nineties, which was the last time Notre Dame was really good. Later I hired another former member of that Holtz Notre Dame staff, Peter Vaas, to replace Cutcliffe. I hired three guys who had been recruiting coordinators: Rob Ianello, our receivers coach and recruiting coordinator, from the University of Wisconsin; Haywood; and Brian Polian, our special-teams coach, from Central Florida.

It is the best coaching staff that has ever been hired over the phone, I promise you that.

If there is one point I constantly stress to my assistant coaches, it is that you can outwork your opponent. Always! That doesn't mean everyone has to work twenty-four hours a day and be ready to drop dead, but you have to be willing to work hard. There's no such thing as nine to five. If that isn't the biggest farce I've ever heard, I don't know what is.

I'm in my office every day, religiously, at four forty-five in the morning. I don't come in any later. I might come in a little earlier if I've had a bad night's sleep, but no later. I like working when I have no one bothering me. I don't answer the phone when it rings. Usually, when someone's calling, he's looking for tickets. My family and very, very dearest friends have the number of my cell phone, which we call the "Bat phone," if they need to get ahold of me.

Another point I make with my assistants is that besides working harder than your opponent, you'd better have integrity. If you don't have that, you can never consider yourself a success. I hate to lose, but win or lose, I do so with integrity. It's important never to give up your morals for the sake of winning. You have to be able to make room for both. I will never run a program where integrity and family aren't just as important as winning.

THE PATRIOTS WOULD finish the 2004 regular season by beating the Jets, on the road, and San Francisco by a combined score of 44–14, answering the question of whether we would hold up with a coordinator splitting his time between two jobs.

Still, it bothered me that the media and fans thought that I was shortchanging the Patriots and shirking my duties with them, because the whole premise in me taking the Notre Dame job was that I was going to finish the job that I had. No one inside the Patriot organization felt that I was throwing in the towel. Not Belichick. Not the players. Not the assistant coaches. Not Mr. Kraft. I think they knew me better than that.

The players know you. The media and the fans don't know you. I always found it humorous when I'd hear, on talk radio in Boston, a fan say, "I don't like Charlie Weis's personality. Romeo Crennel is a nice guy, but that Charlie, he's a jerk."

That fan didn't know me. What he said might be true. I am a miserable person by nature. I'm not happy most of the time. But he didn't know that, because he didn't know me.

Corey Dillon had recovered from his injured hamstring in time for the postseason, and it showed in his performance. He ran for 144 yards in our 20–3 divisional-round playoff win over the Colts to set up another AFC Championship Game, against the Steelers at Pittsburgh. Now we were able to use the game plan we'd had for Pittsburgh the first time, and the outcome was entirely different.

Dillon carried the ball twenty-four times for seventy-three yards. We ran Deion Branch on a reverse for fourteen yards on our first offensive play of the game, which we controlled from the start. That run should have gone for a touchdown, but Troy Polamalu made a phenomenal play. He was behind the line of scrimmage and turned around and ran Branch down from behind. After the Steelers came within fourteen points in the fourth quarter, we ran Branch on the same reverse for a twenty-three-yard touchdown to ice our 41–27 victory and set up our third Super Bowl appearance in four seasons—this one against the Philadelphia Eagles.

Super Bowl XXXIX, in Jackonsville, was a little weird for me. It would be my final game with the Patriots and as a coach in the

NFL. This also would be the second year in a row when the head coach from the other team was one of my closer friends.

I had been friends with Andy Reid for years, as I had been with John Fox. I had talked with Andy once, by phone, two weeks before the game. Then he saw me on the field before the game and he said, "I know, I know. You can't talk to me for more than fifteen seconds or Belichick will have to shoot you."

The media billed it as a showdown between Jim Johnson, the Eagles' defensive coordinator, and me. I didn't think it was such a big showdown. No one on the Patriots did. We thought we had them. We felt that once we figured out what Johnson's plan was going to be, we'd be able to handle it.

As usual, his plan was to blitz on third down; Johnson has always been notorious for that. We took advantage of it in the Super Bowl by throwing a lot of screen passes. Most of the screens we threw worked in that game. Some were different from what we had run in previous games. We were using different personnel and different formations to run the screens, and that was not what the Eagles were expecting us to do in those situations.

They were definitely not expecting what we did when we got the ball back after they scored the first touchdown of the game five minutes into the second quarter. Tommy threw two consecutive screen passes to Dillon, for thirteen and sixteen yards. We had thrown consecutive screen passes before, but that was the first time we had gone "four open"—which is where you have four detached receivers, meaning there's no tight end on the line of scrimmage next to an offensive tackle—from two different personnel groups and run screens on back-to-back plays. The Eagles weren't ready for either play. Although Tommy would end up fumbling on a sack deep in Philadelphia territory, those screens changed the momentum of the game and calmed things down when they could have gotten a little crazy.

We were also throwing screens in predictable situations, such as when they were going to blitz. A screen can sometimes be great in that situation, especially if the defense rolls coverage away from a certain formation set, because you know you're going to get advantageous numbers between blockers and defenders.

One time, early in the fourth quarter, the Eagles were so certain the screen was coming that their defensive coaches and players were yelling before the snap, "Watch the screen! Watch the screen!" However, because the play was in their end of the field, where they showed a tendency to roll the coverage opposite of where the screen was going, we still had the numbers. Tommy threw to Faulk, who picked up fourteen yards to the 2-yard line. Dillon ran for a touchdown on the next play to give us a 21–14 lead.

It took about a quarter for our offense to settle down. Once we did, we were solid in the second and third quarters and consistent enough in the fourth. The Eagles got one late score to make it 24–21, but the game was over by then. The finishing touch came when Rodney Harrison, our veteran safety, intercepted Donovan McNabb with nine seconds left.

Once again Tommy and Deion played phenomenally. Tommy ended up throwing for 236 yards and two touchdowns, finishing with a passer rating of 110.2. Deion caught eleven passes for 133 yards and was voted the game's MVP.

For my wife, the happiest Super Bowl was the first one because it was such an upset. For me, the happiest and most rewarding Super Bowl was the last one because I felt that the people of New England would forever have blamed me if we hadn't won. Now I could leave, walking out a champion and also knowing that the time I'd put into both jobs had paid off on one end, and positive residual effects would show in our recruiting in 2006.

Before the Super Bowl, I never talked with Bill Belichick or Romeo Crennel about it being our final game together, but this was it. After Rodney intercepted that ball, Bill grabbed me and Romeo for a group hug. It doesn't get any better than that. You had three guys who had been together for a lot of years, and now two of us were going on to run our own shows. Romeo was named the Cleveland coach that night. When you go out on top, it's Utopia.

I was emotional after that game. It started to build up when I was hugging Bill and Romeo. Then it built up a little more when I made my usual beeline toward the stands to bring Maura and Charlie down on the field. Finally, when I got to Tommy, I let it out. I was emotionally drained.

Afterward I told him, "You're ready. You might not have been ready a year ago, but you're ready to run this offense without me here. I don't mean call the plays, because the coaches still call the plays, but you don't need the security blanket anymore. I've been the security blanket for you, and you don't need it anymore."

11

One Team + One Voice = Success

My son, Charlie, is my best buddy and biggest critic.

(Courtesy of Michael and Susan Bennett)

"Nice game, Dad. Sloppy second half, huh?"

—Charlie Weis Jr.

I n February of 2005, I didn't pull any punches when I got together with the Notre Dame players for the first time when no one else was around. I let them know that the only way this was going to work was if everyone bought into the team concept. There would be no middle ground. Full buy-in or nothing.

"This is what we're going to do and how we're going to do it," I told them. "If anyone doesn't like it, just quit. Just bag it."

That same month we started having them do conditioning drills two days a week in the twenty-five-thousand-square-foot conditioning center in the Guglielmino Athletics Complex, affectionately known as "the Gug" (pronounced Goog). Under NCAA rules, the players are not allowed to work with footballs at that time. It's all bag drills, cone drills, and everything else you can do without footballs.

For the first two weeks, I walked around with a clipboard. The coaches wore the usual coaching gear; I was in my usual business attire, wearing a shirt and tie. I was not leading the drills. I was just trying to learn the players. What I saw was that they were in crummy shape. What I heard was their bitching about how tough it was or yelling at a teammate who screwed up rather than helping him through a particular drill. It was just complain, complain, complain. There were excuses all over the place.

For two weeks, I didn't say one word. I just took notes. On Monday night, before the third Tuesday of the conditioning drills, I got all of the players together in a meeting room. I told them, "Starting tomorrow, things are changing. I will not be in a shirt and tie. I'll be in sweats. I'll have a whistle. And things are changing."

That was all I said. Then I walked out of the room.

The next day, they were mine. The clipboard was gone, as was the tie. I had a whistle around my neck and I was unmerciful. I was ruthless. I was on them and on them and on them and on them and on them and on them, from the time I blew the whistle for the start until the time I blew it for the end. I was killing them verbally, criticizing everything they did. To the ones who kept bitching and complaining, I said, "Why don't you just quit? Just quit." I planted the seed, figuring that if any players were going to walk away, that would be the time they were thinking about it.

I kept the pressure on through that entire off-season. There is a famous sign posted outside our locker room in Notre Dame Stadium, on the stairway leading down to the tunnel to the field. In blue letters on a gold background, it says, "Play Like a Champion Today." In March of 2005, before we left the locker room for the first practice of spring ball, I looked at that sign. Then I turned to the players and said, "See that sign? I have a problem with that sign. We're not going on the game field today. We're going over to the practice fields. You should play like a champion every day, not just on Saturdays when you walk out on that game field."

I tried to run off as many of them as I could because if they weren't going to buy into the team, I wanted them gone. We started out with eighty-five kids. About seven or eight did quit right off the bat. I didn't care. I was prepared to go into the season with fifty if I had to. By the time we got to training camp in the first week of August, we were into the low seventies. We could have had more guys quit, but a couple of them rallied themselves.

The next thing you have to do is teach everyone what his role is and that he has to be willing to accept what it is. I dress a hundred guys on game day. I'm never going to play a hundred guys, but letting players wear the uniform the day of the game is a reward for what they've done during the week. For a lot of those guys, their only role is to go out and get beat up in practice every day while trying to simulate the teams we're going to be playing against. That is their job. If they're not willing to accept that role, then they don't need to be there.

In sports, there are many people that are selfish. Once you can get people to not think selfishly, to suppress their egos and to focus on how they can make the team better, success can be achieved. The team is always supposed to be more important than the individual. It should always speak with one voice. How many opinions do you think count with Bill Parcells? Right. His. How many opinions do you think count with Bill Belichick? Right again. Do you think Andy Reid cares about anyone else's opinion? What about John Fox? Bill Cowher? Mike Holmgren? They don't care, because all they're worrying about is the team. They know that the only way the team can be successful is if everyone's on the same page.

I'll be the first to admit that when I was an assistant coach, I would bitch about Parcells and Belichick not letting their assistants talk to the media even though players were free to do so. I felt that they didn't trust what we would say and that they believed the only reason you wanted to talk to the media was to self-promote. What I've come to find out is that while the media look at a head coach who puts a gag order on assistants as a negative, there are a lot of pros that come with such a policy. Often, things can be misconstrued when multiple people are talking about the same subject. Parcells and Belichick have always felt that there is one leader of the team, and his is the only voice that everyone should hear from the coaching staff.

As a head coach, I'm more liberal than they are when it comes to assistant coaches dealing with the media. I understand why Parcells and Belichick won't allow assistants to be interviewed right after a game. They might not have seen the same thing that we saw. Consequently, they might say one thing and we might say something else. I always felt, though, that once I spoke with the head coach about the questions to anticipate, I would be smart enough not to say something stupid during the week. Not that it mattered. Those rules were set in stone.

The media policy I have for our coaching staff is as follows: On game day, no assistants are allowed to speak with reporters; I do all of the talking in my postgame news conference. On Sunday, after I've had a chance to review videotape of the game, I have a more expansive news conference to cover what happened on Saturday. On Sunday and Monday, I'll talk with the entire staff about what they can and cannot say to the media about the upcoming opponent; they are never allowed to speak about the previous game.

Reporters can request the assistants they would like to interview on the designated days of their availability, beginning with offensive coaches on Tuesday, followed by defensive coaches on Wednesday, and special-teams coaches on Thursday. Usually, reporters ask only for the coordinators, but sometimes they might want to speak with the assistant head coach on offense and the assistant head coach on defense. They ask for these guys hoping that they're going to get more information than I give them. They won't get it very often. When they do, they'll get it only once because that sort of thing can cause division. Parcells used to call it "division from within."

You always have to remember that it's not about you. It's about winning championships. Somewhere along the line, the goal of the team has to become more important than the goal of the individual. That is easier said than done. There are very few coaches, on any level of sport, who can consistently get their players to suppress their egos and put the team ahead of them. Parcells and Belichick found a way to take a bunch of guys that were making zillions of dollars and get them to buy into the team-first mentality. I would say that's a pretty good reason to implement their philosophy regardless of whom you're coaching.

EVEN IN THE one-voice, one-opinion approach, there is an opportunity for every player on the team to feel that he can be heard. In addition to our three captains—who for 2006 were Brady Quinn on offense, Tommy Zbikowski on defense, and Travis Thomas on special teams—I established what I call a "leadership" committee. The committee has a representative from each position who can speak to one of the captains on behalf of all of the other players at his position. The captain then comes to me with whatever is on the mind of a particular position group.

I very seldom agree with anything they say, but I'm always willing and able to listen to them. One rule: No bitching allowed. For instance, I don't want to hear any complaints about having a full-pads practice on Wednesday, which I normally don't do. If anyone bitches about it, I'll have us in full pads on Thursday, too.

The players also do a good job of policing themselves. The boss can't handle all of the problems. Sometimes the problem has to be handled by the team, not the head coach. In '05, I received a request through the leadership committee to make bars off-limits to players on Thursday night, as well as Friday night, before a Saturday game. In college, Thursday night is a big drinking night, and there were members of the committee who thought it was hurting the team's ability to be prepared and ready to go on Saturday. I went along with the request until there was one issue during the year that happened on a night other than Thursday or Friday. After that, players weren't allowed to be in bars on any nights during the season.

I give them the noose and let them hang themselves. I'll start off giving them some freedom. As soon as they give me the opportunity to tighten the noose, I tighten it . . . and I tighten it again . . . and again . . . and again. I try to treat them like men, not like kids, because I let them dictate how tight I'm going to make that noose.

That goes for assistant coaches, too. I don't have many rules, but if you break one, you're going to have serious problems with me. I had a young guy on my staff—an assistant to an assistant to an assistant—who decided he was going to go out and have a couple of beers one night. When he came in late to a meeting the next morning, I told him, "If I hear about you being in any bar or any restaurant that has a bar in South Bend for the next six months, you're fired. So you'd better start enjoying yourself at McDonald's and Wendy's, because every place else is off-limits."

As the head coach, you're the CEO. Everyone is looking to you for leadership and guidance, on and off the field. For example, I will never have a beer or any other alcoholic beverage in public. If I don't know somebody, I will not drink with him. When my staff's out, that doesn't hold for them. I'll take my assistant coaches out to a restaurant for dinner, and if they want to have a couple of drinks, they can do so. I can't. I'm setting the example. If you can't set the example and you're setting the rules, there's a conflict. There's a contradiction.

Everything you do and say as a head coach starts with putting pressure on yourself. My feeling is, once I've taken the blame and put the pressure on myself, I feel free to "spread the wealth" in private. I always take the blame publicly. Behind closed doors, it might not be exactly the same.

The team-first concept doesn't stop with the players or coaches. I've preached the same thing to the rest of the students because they're part of the team too. After I was hired, I was asked by some of the student body if I would speak to the students at all twenty-six dorms on campus. I agreed. The way we did it was to combine the dorms so that there were double the students for each appearance and I could schedule thirteen nightly speaking engagements from ten fifteen to eleven o'clock. Each dorm would be packed wall to wall with students. You couldn't squeeze another body in the room.

The main point I made was that they couldn't be bandwagon fans—the kind who are with you when you're winning and everything is going well and who are just as quick to turn against you when you're struggling—and expect the football team to respond in a positive way. I knew what I was talking about, because I had gone to school there. I had been one of those bandwagon fans. I was the one who, during my sophomore year, had taken my complaint about the team all the way to the school president.

"I'm no different from you," I told them. "I wasn't a player. I was a student, just like you. I went to all of the games, just like you. I felt I was part of the team, just like you. Being part of the team means taking ownership of the team. If you want to take ownership of this team, you have to start acting that way. You can't be bandwagon fans.

"You have to be supportive all the time, not just some of the time. You're either with us or you're not with us."

I would always leave the last ten minutes for questions after giving them one ground rule: "Do not ask me about last year's team. I was not here last year. I could not answer any question about last year intelligently. I'll talk with you about the here and now. I will not talk with you about last year."

Sure enough, somewhere along the line, someone would ask me to compare the way I did something with the way Coach Willingham did it. I would look at everyone with my New Jersey smart-ass look. Then I would look at the person who asked the question and say, "Did you listen to a word I said?"

Every once in a while there'd be a typical fan who asked a question but was already giving the answer before I had a chance to respond. My favorite reply would be, "So, how, with all of your football expertise, did you come to that deduction?"

It would be a very humbling experience. I'd usually end up humiliating a whole bunch of students, but when I finished the series of talks I felt a much stronger connection with the whole student body.

OUR '05 OPENER was against the University of Pittsburgh, coached by former Dolphins and Bears head coach Dave Wannstedt, at Heinz Field in Pittsburgh. Nine months earlier I had been in that same stadium when the Patriots beat the Steelers to advance to Super Bowl XXXIX.

Like me, Wannstedt was coaching his first game for his alma mater. To help celebrate his return, Pitt brought back an impressive group of alumni. Dan Marino, Tony Dorsett, and Mike Ditka were all there. I had gone against Dave many times in the NFL. When we prepared for the University of Pittsburgh, I was attacking the Dolphins' scheme. Regardless of the level of competition, coaches don't change their stripes. They are what they are.

I felt a lot better after the game than I did beforehand, and not only because of our 42–21 victory that saw Brady Quinn lead touchdown drives on five of our first six possessions. There had been a lot of naysayers predicting we were going to lose every game, beginning with that one. Mark May and Lee Corso, college football analysts for ESPN, said we were going to start the season 0–6 or 1–5. (Incidentally, I have a videotape copy of them making those predictions that I've replayed to my team many times.) Even though we were on the road, and Pitt was ranked twenty-third in the country and we weren't ranked in the top twenty-five, I expected us to win. My expectations were higher than everyone else's.

Well, almost everyone else's. The exception was my son, Charlie, who was twelve at the time. Now besides being my best buddy, he also is my biggest critic. He stands right with me on the sidelines for every game, home and away. Several times he has asked me, and not nicely, "Why did you call that?" As we walked off the field in Pittsburgh, with me feeling pretty good that we had just won our opener, Charlie said, "Nice game, Dad. Sloppy second half, huh?"

Our second game, also on the road, was against No. 3 Michigan. We won that, too, to take a 2–0 record into our home opener against Michigan State. We came back from a twenty-one-point deficit, pushed the game to overtime, but ended up losing, 44–41. I screwed up that game a little bit. Before we faced Pitt and Michigan, I played up the winning-on-the-road and us-against-the-world angles so much that I even got into the idea of how playing at home was a distraction. I think the players bought into that angle so much that we were flat in the first half against Michigan State.

In the past, Notre Dame's players would have been talking about what a "great comeback" they made. I made sure I killed that notion as soon as we got to the locker room after the game.

"Comeback, my ass!" I said. "We lost a game. There's no such thing as 'great' when you lose. Let's get that straight around here. You're going to walk out there and listen to the media telling you how great a comeback you had. That's a bunch of crap. The bottom line, fellas, is we lost."

I think they learned as much from that game as from any other game we played. They were starting to get it. About halfway through spring ball they had begun to realize that things were different, that they would be held more accountable, and that anything short of winning just wasn't good enough anymore.

- - -

NO EXCUSES

BEFORE THE NEXT game, versus Washington, I had an unforgettable experience. There was a kid who lived just outside of South Bend named Montana Mazurkiewicz. He'd had cancer for sixteen months, and was dying. His mother had contacted me to see if I would go over to the house to visit with the kid because he had only a couple of weeks to live.

I went over to his house, and as soon as I saw him, I knew this kid wasn't going to last two weeks. In fact, later on, when I walked out of the house, I called my wife with watery eyes and said, "Honey, this kid isn't going to last two days."

I let the kid verbally abuse me about the Michigan State game, like any ten-year-old kid would. Then I asked him, "What can I do for you?"

"Coach, I have an inoperable tumor," Montana said. "They're telling me I'm only going to last a couple of weeks. I just want to last long enough to see your game against Washington on Saturday because I want to see you beat Coach Willingham."

I looked at the kid, trying to fight back the tears. "I'll tell you what," I said. "Why don't you call the first play of the game?"

Now, what is any ten-year-old boy in America going to call? He's going to call a pass. Montana didn't ask for us to throw just any pass, though. He asked for us to throw the pass to the right side of our offense.

"You've got it," I said.

After we arrived in Washington, I received a phone call. Montana had died.

Given what I had seen when I visited his house, I can't say I was surprised by the news. Still, something like that jolts you, especially when you're talking about a ten-year-old kid. I called his mother, and after offering my condolences, I said, "Well, we're still calling the play in memory of your son."

The Huskies got the ball first. They drove almost the length of the field and then fumbled. We recovered . . . at our six-inch line. Brady Quinn knew about the promise I had made to the kid. He also probably knew that throwing the ball might not necessarily be the automatic choice I would make from our own six-inch line.

"Well, Coach, this is why they pay you big bucks," Quinn said. "What are we going to do?"

"We're calling the play," I said. "We've got no other choice."

It wasn't about doing what was right for the situation from a football perspective. It was about honoring Montana's wish. I had made a promise to him, so although it might cost us, I felt that I had a debt to pay. I owed it to Montana and to his family even though he wasn't around to see it.

Our tight end, Anthony Fasano, also knew about the promise because he was the one who would be catching the ball. After Quinn ran onto the field, Fasano asked him, "Is it still on?"

"It's still on," Quinn said.

Quinn threw the pass to Fasano. It gained thirteen yards. We never punted until there were eleven seconds left in the game, which we won, 36–17.

I have two regrets about the whole experience. The first, of course, was that Montana didn't last long enough to see it. The second came after we returned to South Bend. As far as I was concerned, this was supposed to have been a private thing. All of a sudden, during my regular press conference the next day, I got bombarded with questions about Montana.

It turned out that his mom had called up all of the local TV stations to tell them what we had done. Now it was a national story.

A lopsided win at Purdue gave us a 4–1 record and No. 9 ranking for our always much-anticipated game against USC. The Trojans were undefeated. They were No. 1 in the country. They were averaging fifty-one points per game. And you know what? I thought we were going to win. I was confident that we could win. I was so confident that I had us bring in several recruits, many of the best high school players in the country, for official visits that weekend. People around the school thought we were nuts because if we got blown out, none of the recruits would want to come to Notre Dame.

We pulled out all of the stops for this one. We had Joe Montana, Tim Brown, Chris Zorich, and Rudy Ruettiger at the Friday night pep rally, which drew forty-five thousand people, about thirty-four thousand more than usual. The rally is usually in the Joyce Center, but because of the crowd I moved it into the stadium. I got on the public-address system and taunted the crowd a little bit about how much noise it was capable of making during the game.

"They all tell me that this is a quiet place to play, that you don't make any noise around here," I said, prompting boos. "Well, when we're on offense, be quiet. When we're on defense, that's when you make noise." The crowd appreciated my Jersey sarcasm and began cheering as loudly as it could, which was pretty loudly.

We even wore our kelly green jerseys, but not until after we warmed up in our blue ones. I had planned on us wearing the green jerseys all week, but the players didn't find out about it until after they got back to the locker room after warm-ups and found them hanging in their lockers. The players went bananas when they saw them. We had worn the green jerseys against USC when I was a senior at Notre Dame. When reporters asked me all week long if we were going to break them in the first game I coached against the Trojans, I said, "Come on." I didn't say no. I just said, "Come on." You bring out the green jerseys when you're an underdog, playing against the best team in the country. That was the situation. That was what I did.

When I was on the field during pregame warm-ups, I saw Sean Salisbury, the NFL analyst for ESPN and an alumnus of USC.

"We're going to win this game," I told him.

"I'm afraid you actually believe that," he said.

"I do believe it."

"I know you do."

I thought that we could control the tempo of the game, slowing it down because the Trojans had too much offensive firepower. I thought that our offense could move the ball against their defense and score enough to win the game.

My confidence seemed well placed in the first quarter when I went for it on fourth down from our own 20-yard line. All we needed was six inches. I felt that we could get six inches, and we did, on a keeper by Quinn. We wound up driving for our first touchdown of the game. If we hadn't made that first down, I would have been a dumb-ass. We made it. I thought we could more than hold our own offensively. We did.

USC took a 28–24 lead in the fourth quarter when Reggie Bush ran for his third touchdown of the game. We came back with an eighty-seven-yard touchdown drive to recapture the lead with about two minutes left. The Trojans got the ball again. We sacked Matt Leinart on second down. On third-and-nineteen, they gained ten. Then, on fourth-and-nine, Leinart threw a fade up the sidelines twenty-four yards to a well-covered Dwayne Jarrett, who ran thirty-seven more yards to put USC at our 13-yard line. The cornerback, Ambrose Wooden, was right there, but Leinart actually put the ball under Wooden's elbow and into Jarrett's hands. It was a great throw by Leinart.

Four plays later Leinart scrambled from inside the 5, tried hurling himself toward the end zone, and fell short. The ball got knocked out of bounds as the clock ran out. I put my hands in the air, thinking we had won. A lot of the fans, thinking the same thing, came rushing onto the field. There was only one problem. The game wasn't over. The officials put seven seconds back on the clock and were correct in doing so. They also placed the ball inside the 1.

In college football, you play by the rules of the visiting team's conference, which, in the case of USC, was the Pac-10. Notre Dame is an independent, and we use Big Ten rules on the road. The Pac-10 has an instant-replay system to review calls, but it is up to the visiting coach to decide beforehand whether it will be used in the game. I always elect to use replay when we're on the road. For whatever reason, Pete Carroll didn't want to use it. Therefore, there was no way of determining for sure whether the ball was spotted right. The replay that I saw from NBC's coverage seemed to show that the ball should have been back about two or three yards to the 3- or 4-yard line.

Still, the bottom line is that the Trojans decided to go for it. If they didn't get in, the game would be over and we would win. Leinart kept it, Bush pushed him into the end zone, and USC won, 34–31. A lot of Notre Dame fans made a big deal about Bush getting away with pushing Leinart. I didn't make a big deal about it because I thought it was a heads-up play. Unfortunately, we lost.

In the locker room, our players were all feeling sorry for themselves because it was a disheartening loss. We had put everything into this game. It was worse than the Michigan State game.

We had even used the green jerseys. A bunch of guys, including Wooden, felt that they were individually responsible for the outcome.

"Quit feeling sorry for yourselves," I told the team. "We all lost this game. There's no one individual that lost it. We had plenty of opportunities to close out this game. We could have done it on offense. We could have done it on defense. We could have done it on special teams. I can cite five examples right now of things I screwed up during the game and tell you why I lost it too. You lose as a team just like you win as a team. So quit feeling sorry for yourselves.

"And I can tell you this, fellas. You have five regular-season games left and you will not lose again. You've lost your last regular-season game. We're going to win all five of those games, and then we're going to play in a bowl, and I don't mean the Tangerine Bowl or the Astro-Bluebonnet Bowl."

I wasn't just saying what I said to make those guys feel better about themselves. I meant every word of it. I honestly believed we could win out and play in a major bowl game. We had just taken the best team in the country to the wire. We were obviously a lot better than everyone thought we were. But not better than I thought we were—I thought we should have been 6–0 at the time.

After addressing the media, then talking with a couple of players one-on-one to make sure they weren't too far in the tank, I sat in my office for a minute with my son. I got up and said, "Come on, Charlie. We're taking a walk."

"Where are we going?" he asked.

"We're going over to USC's locker room."

"Why are we going over there?"

"We're going to go congratulate them."

"For what?"

"For a hell of a game, Charlie."

He walked over with me to the USC locker room. As the opposing coach, I didn't want to just walk right in uninvited, so we stopped at the door. At about the same time, Leinart and Bush were heading back from talking with the media and spotted me standing there. I exchanged hugs with both of them and told them, "Great game." Pete wasn't there at the time, so I asked Leinart and Bush for permission to say something to their team. They said I could.

"Shut up, fellas!" Bush yelled. "The coach from Notre Dame's here."

"I just want to congratulate you," I said. "That was a hell of a game, a hard-fought battle. I hope you win out."

It was hard, but it was something I had to do. I turned around and walked out. I didn't wait around for claps or kudos or anything like that. I returned to my office and sat down with Charlie.

"Why did you do that?" he asked.

"Charlie, I wanted to teach you a lesson," I said. "It's easy to be a good winner. It's really easy. Everyone acts well when they win. Don't get me wrong. It's never good to lose, but there's a certain way you should act when you lose. You should show as much class when you lose as when you win. It's much more difficult to do, but you have to do it."

Afterward, I gave the following orders to the team: No player was allowed to talk about the USC game or any game in the first half of the season. When I spoke with the media the Tuesday after we played USC, I said we were beginning our "second season" and explained how we had broken our season in half. We were getting ready to play our "home opener" of the second half on Saturday against Brigham Young. We would be doing so as the ninth-ranked team in the country.

BYU came out blitzing us on every down, and we took advantage of it. In the first half, Quinn was 25-of-30 for a school-record 287 yards. As I walked off the field at halftime, with us holding a 21–10 lead, the sideline reporter for NBC asked me, "When are you going to get the running game going?" I looked at him and said, "If they're going to keep bringing it, we're going to keep slinging it."

I don't know if that was the answer he wanted to hear, but we stayed true to that plan. They kept bringing it and we kept slinging it. Quinn finished 32-of-41 for 467 yards and a school-record six touchdown passes in our 49–23 victory.

WE FOLLOWED THAT game by beating Tennessee, 41–21. Next up, Navy. At the pep rally on the night before the game, I got on the microphone and talked about how I wanted our student body and fans to show respect to the Naval Academy.

"When they come out tomorrow, instead of booing them, the way most colleges do, stand up and cheer for them," I said. "Regardless of the outcome of the game, I want you to respect their team."

A great tradition when service academies finish playing a game is that their players walk over to their student section and sing their alma mater with the students. Before the game, I asked Paul Johnson, Navy's coach, if as a sign of respect, our players could stand behind his players when they sang the Navy alma mater after the game—win or lose.

"Fine," he said.

I think Coach Johnson was surprised because I don't think he had gotten that request before. Then I told our captains that in the fourth quarter, I would inform the entire team about what we were going to do.

It was probably one of the things I have felt best about doing as a head coach. The guys at Navy and the other service academies are not just college football players. When they finish playing, they have a minimum five-year commitment to go defend our country. That deserved our respect, which we gave them after our 42–21 victory.

That win nudged us up the national rankings from No. 7 to No. 6. When we beat Syracuse, 34–10, to improve our record to 8–2, we set up what could best be described as a high-stakes situation at Stanford. If we won, we got a Bowl Championship Series bid, Notre Dame's first in five years. If we lost, we didn't. That made it a fifteen-million-dollar game because that would be what the school would receive for playing in a BCS game.

Stanford took the lead, 31–30, with under two minutes to go in the game. A touchback started us at our 20. You want to talk about a pressure drive? That was a pressure drive. The first play was a classic example of drawing one up in the dirt. We called a pass that we had not called since facing Michigan in the second game of the year, because I felt it gave us the best chance to get a chunk of yardage and put us in plus territory quickly. With the time remaining and our field position, we couldn't afford to dink and dunk our way down there. Maurice Stovall was running a go route and Jeff Samardzija was running a crossing route. I told Brady Quinn, "Take a look at Stovall. If he's there, lay it up to him. If not, buy a little time and hit Samardzija on the crossing route." He hit Samardzija for thirty-two yards on the crossing route to put us at the Stanford 48-yard line.

Quinn followed that up with a hitch adjustment route to Stovall for another twenty yards, and we were deep in Stanford territory pretty quickly. I put in multiple tight ends to pound it in there. With fifty-five seconds left, Darius Walker ran six yards for a touchdown, and then he took a direct snap and ran for the two-point conversion to give us a 38–31 win and the BCS bid.

This two-minute drive reminded me of Tommy Brady. There are a lot of similarities between Brady Quinn and Tommy Brady. Confidence. Leadership. Intelligence. Arm. By the way, they're both "pretty boys." I've seen all of the quarterbacks in the NFL in recent years. With the exception of Tommy Brady and Peyton Manning, you'd be hard-pressed not to want this kid, more than any other quarterback, on your team.

WE SCORED RIGHT off the bat in our Fiesta Bowl game at Sun Devil Stadium in Tempe, Arizona, against Ohio State. We went right down the field to the first of three touchdown runs by Walker. The Buckeyes had a bunch of big plays, finishing with more than six hundred yards in offense. They hit a couple of long passes. Teddy Ginn Jr. ran a reverse sixty-eight yards for a touchdown.

Still, we cut Ohio State's lead to 27–20 on an eighty-yard scoring drive with about five and a half minutes to go in the game. The Buckeyes took over. I had made up my mind that if we could prevent them from scoring, get the ball back, and get another touchdown, we were going for two. We would try to win the game outright. That went against my principles: in that situation, I would normally play for overtime and try to win it then. But I felt that if we could come back from being fourteen points down, we had to go for it all. I even knew the play I wanted to call for the two-point conversion.

I never got the chance. Troy Smith, Ohio State's quarterback, completed passes to convert two third-and-long situations. After the second one, Antonio Pittman had a run to the left that busted for a sixty-yard touchdown, and that was the game.

I had expected us to win, but the Buckeyes were the better team that day. They were coached better and played better. I never judge a game by saying one team has better athletes than the other. You've got to go by what happens on game day.

Their coaching staff and their team did a better job than our coaching staff and team.

12

Dome Sweet Dome

There isn't a better home team in the world than the one I have with Hannah, Maura, and Charlie. *(Courtesy of Michael and Susan Bennett)*

"9–3 IS NOT GOOD ENOUGH"

—Sign in the Notre Dame weight room

When I was approached for the Notre Dame job, Maura, Charlie, and I started talking about what this could mean to our family. Maura hadn't gone to Notre Dame. Charlie had followed it some but only because he saw that I followed it some. They didn't understand the magnitude of what this move would mean to our family life. They didn't understand that all of us, not just me, were going to be embraced by the whole university and the whole town. Not everyone would recognize them walking down the street, but everyone would know of Maura Weis, and everyone would know of Charlie and Hannah Weis.

I explained to Maura and Charlie that if we could get a reasonable compensation package, our lives would be a lot better than they would be with me in the pros, for two big reasons. Number one, the NCAA's twenty-hour rule allows a coach to be with his athletes for only twenty hours per week during the season. I would be spending more time at home. Number two, we were going to be living in a town rather than a major metropolitan area. We were going to be at the heart of the whole university.

It sounded as good to them as it sounded to me. Charlie was ready for me to take a head-coaching job. He had been ready for three years. Even though he had a couple of close friends in New England, he was primed for us to make a move. Maura was too. She wasn't caught up in the idea of changing scenery, but she felt strongly that I deserved an opportunity to be a head coach.

Now that I've taken the job, my wife and son have enjoyed it almost more than I've enjoyed it. We go to many home basketball games, sitting right at midcourt. We go to hockey games. We go to baseball games. My wife and children are a part of the community. They're a part of the university. They feel like they belong.

In the pros, with all of the time you spend with your players and all of your prep time for games, you don't see your family very much from the start of training camp through the end of the season. In college, from four forty-five in the morning until two thirty in the afternoon, I have no players, as they are in class. In the pros, you're meeting with the players from seven o'clock in the morning until six o'clock at night. In college, the greatest amount of time I spend away from home is when I'm recruiting, but the trips aren't too bad. It's four solid weeks of travel. Once you're done with it, you don't do it again until the next year.

I have a deal with my family. I will give them every second of my time away from work. I don't play golf. I don't fish. I don't go out with the boys. Except for the trip I take each summer with my longtime buddies from Jersey to Monmouth Park, I don't spend

one second of time on myself, because I'm spending a dispropor-
tionate amount of time on football in relationship to my family.

In 2006, we built a home in Granger, Indiana. It's on an eight-
acre lot that includes an indoor and outdoor riding arena and
stables for the two horses that Maura owns. She used to board
them an hour and fifteen minutes away. In the back is a baseball
diamond for Charlie. It's his "Field of Dreams."

Charlie would love to play major-league baseball one day. I
have a feeling he'll end up in sports in some capacity, whether it's
owning a sporting goods store, being a sports announcer, or maybe
even coaching. He has paid attention to what I've been doing his
whole life. He studies the NFL draft. He has taken a strong interest in what's involved with being a football coach.

During my second stint with the Patriots, Charlie was fortunate enough to settle into one school for five years. Now, for the
first time, he actually sees a vision of the rest of his life. He sees
himself going to a high school in Indiana for four years and then
going to Notre Dame. He already has dinner once a week in the
South Dining Hall.

The thing Charlie's trying to differentiate is whether kids are
friends with him because of him or because of me. I think that
he's finally starting to get a little hold of that one. A person who
has been able to help him a great deal on that count is Tim Mc-
Donnell, my quality-control guy and right-hand man. Tim is from
the Mara family, which owns half of the New York Giants. You
think there might have been a few "friends" along the way who
liked Tim as much for the potential of being hooked up with Giants tickets as they did for Tim?

At thirteen, Charlie doesn't want to listen to everything we have to say. We talk with him about things like drugs, drinking, and the like, but he can relate better to someone like Tim, who is closer in age and who can communicate with him on a different level than my wife and I can.

During the 2005 season, a bunch of Notre Dame students from New Jersey started selling T-shirts—in my honor but without my permission—that said, "Charlie's Army." When my son saw the T-shirts, it gave him an idea for us to do something good. Now there's another T-shirt for sale. On the front it says, "Charlie Jr.'s Army Reserve." On the back it says, "Play Like a Champion Every Day," going back to the theme I established on the first day of spring ball in '05. All of the profits from the sales of those shirts go to Hannah and Friends.

Hannah's eleven and a fifth-grader who has fit in nicely at her school. She's involved in a recreation program outside of school called Champs, which provides social events for people with special needs. Hannah is involved in the bowling and music programs.

Maura has plenty of help in caring for Hannah. Hannah has a live-in "big sister" in Joanna Bond, whom we sponsor as a student at Indiana University South Bend. Sharon Bui, our South Bend director of Hannah and Friends, also has a close relationship with Hannah. Sharon is a "Double Domer," meaning she has two degrees from Notre Dame, and is a rah-rah fan of the university's sports teams. She tries to teach Hannah to say, "Touchdown!" and "Go, Irish!"

Hannah has her own word for hungry that we finally learned after years—it sounds like "ko-kwait"—and she does use some sign language. However, there are a lot of words she speaks clearly. When she wants to listen to music, she'll say, "Music." When she wants to watch videos, she'll say, "Videos." When she has to go to the bathroom, she says, "Bathroom." When she's thirsty, she'll say, "Juice." When she's hungry, she'll go right down the line of her favorite foods: "Chicken . . . cake . . . baked potato . . . raisins . . . cookie . . . M&M's . . . peanuts . . . apple." She'll be nodding her head the whole time, trying to get you into a trance. If you say "No," she'll just go on to the next thing and continue to nod her head until you give in.

Hannah has what we call the "Hannah Magic." Even though she's not very verbal, she knows how to manipulate everyone so she can get what she wants. She has learned very well how to use the word "no" while emphatically shaking her head from side to side. As Hannah has gotten older, it has become her favorite answer to almost every question. If I walk into her room when she's watching videos or listening to music and she doesn't want me in there, she gets up off the floor, pushes me to the door, and says, "See you later." Then she slams the door. One thing Hannah cannot say, though, is "sick." When she doesn't feel well, she just lies down, and you have to figure out on your own that she's sick.

When she goes to bed, which is usually before Charlie, I'll always tell her, "Night-night." She'll respond with "Night-night." Then I'll tell her, "I love you." She'll say, "Love you." That's my favorite conversation with Hannah.

DURING OUR FIRST bye of the '05 season, Kevin White, Notre Dame's director of athletics, talked with me generally about the future and how things were going. He brought up the topic of extending my contract. It didn't surprise me, since there were some NFL teams already inquiring about my possible availability after my first season. I also didn't care one way or the other about doing an extension at that point. I was the head coach of Notre Dame, and I didn't want to start talking about my contract. I was much more concerned with winning games and recruiting players for the future.

"That's why I have an agent," I told Kevin. "If you want to talk about an extension, you need to contact Bob LaMonte. If there is any reason for me to get involved after that, the only day that would happen is on October 24, the Monday after our second bye."

Over the next several weeks, Kevin and Bob went back and forth in negotiations before they finally settled on something they were ready to present to me. Sure enough, at the close of business on October 24, I had a package sitting on my desk with the offer. I brought it home and sat down to look it over with Maura and Charlie.

"Okay, here it is," I said. "What do you want to do?"

They started talking it over. Counting the 2005 season, it amounted to an eleven-year deal. It was for a lot of money, all guaranteed.

"Now, Charlie, let me just tell you something," I said. "If I were to go back in the NFL, I could double this offer."

"Dad, how much money do we need?" Charlie said.

Maura and Charlie wanted to take the deal. Bob thought I should take it too. I didn't even put my vote in because there already was a majority in favor of it.

When I took the Notre Dame job, I said I would be there until Charlie graduated from Notre Dame. The contract extension will allow me to do that. Moreover, with how the contract was reworded, it now became highly unlikely that I would ever go back to the NFL. Not to go into dollar figures, but what once would have been a nominal buyout for an NFL franchise to hire me is now substantial. Therefore, the contract helped recruiting because it eliminated the negative recruiting that people from other schools would do when they would tell a player, "Don't go to Notre Dame with Weis because he's heading back to the NFL."

Notre Dame's high academic standards and our desire to have all of our players graduate make the scope of our recruiting different from that of a lot of other places. It forces us to recruit nationally. By "us," I am including myself. I'd say less than a handful of Division I head coaches recruit all the time. The rest would rather leave it to their assistants. I've been to high schools from Miami, Florida, to Seattle, Washington, and from Mission Viejo, California, to Boston, Massachusetts. You might be in the middle of nowhere or you might be in the middle of a city. The problem is, some of the other good Division I head coaches are out there. You see Pete Carroll all of the time. You see Urban Meyer all of the time. Ron Zook's out there all of the time.

I believe that I have to be out there because I'm the face that people are going to associate with Notre Dame. When I walk into a high school, it's different than when an assistant walks into a high school, because the students know who I am. I think it's a very valuable presence. It doesn't mean the kids are saying yes, but when they see the head coach it makes an impact, since most of the time they're seeing assistant coaches. Of course, I will admit that I walked into one school and the only reason anyone knew me there was because I had worked for the Patriots. They didn't even know I was working at Notre Dame.

The NCAA allows you to have only seven coaches on the road

at one time, so it's always six of our nine assistants—who vary depending on the area or the position of the player we're checking out—and me on the road during a four-week stretch from late April through late May to look at the recruits who will be seniors the following fall. The assistants end up being on the road a total of three weeks. I'm on the road for all four weeks. How can I send my assistants on the road for nearly a month and ask them to bust their butt if I'm not willing to do it myself? I've always believed that you can't ask somebody to work harder than you do. As the leader, you're supposed to work the hardest.

In May, you can initiate one phone call to a recruit. On the other hand, recruits can call you as many times as they want. They can call you every day if they want to. There are recruits I talk to several times in a week.

We set up a board listing high school juniors and rising seniors, by position, in the order we want them. It's almost like a draft board that each team in the NFL sets up, only ours contains high school kids instead of college prospects. We have them graded in four categories: the ones we definitely want, the guys we think we might want, the guys we probably don't want, and the guys we definitely don't want. Even though there are players on our board that will never wear one of our uniforms, they will end up going somewhere else, and we want to keep track of that as well. We keep information on our computers on kids who are younger than juniors, but they are not on our board.

When recruiting, we place equal value on character, academics, and ability. Almost every high school coach in America will tell you a player is a great kid, so you have to do your due diligence. That doesn't mean we're going to know every single thing there is to know on all of them. It isn't like we have police scanners, as the

NFL does. We don't hire the FBI to do background checks. But we do all we can to find out about a kid's character.

You go into the schools and talk with the principals, talk with the guidance counselors, talk with the teachers. You go to the people who will give you the scoop. Maybe that person is the trainer. Maybe that person is the school nurse. It varies from school to school. Some schools don't have a full-time trainer, but you might walk into one school that does, and you visit with him in the training room and he wants to give you all of the answers. At one school in Oklahoma the security guard was the guy who had his finger on the pulse of the whole school.

You end up in the football coach's office, but you look to talk with other people along the way to try to get a broader perspective on the kid. Not that high school coaches are there to lie, but usually they don't have any problems with the kid, because they're the ones giving him the opportunity to play. More often than not, the problems are going to surface in other places around the school. Remember, not all of these kids have the best lives in the whole world. If everyone comes back saying, "This is your type of guy," you're usually on the right track.

Then, of course, we need to find kids that we know are going to graduate. The goal at Notre Dame is for every kid to graduate regardless of race, creed, or color. It doesn't make a difference. That's why our graduation rate is so high; in 2006, Notre Dame was one of six Division I schools whose football program achieved a graduation rate of 90 percent or better. That's why we're up at the top in NCAA academic progress rate (APR), which measures a school's success in retaining scholarship athletes and keeping them eligible in each sport.

Everyone who comes to Notre Dame intends to graduate. The

kids who leave our program after a couple of years are usually transferring to a school that is easier academically or provides an easier chance of them playing. Other than that, everyone stays at Notre Dame and everyone graduates. Obviously, in conjunction with those two things, you need guys who can play football at a high level. It doesn't make any difference if you can read and write and you're a good kid if you can't play.

When I took the job, a lot of people told me that you couldn't get enough good football players at Notre Dame. That's a fallacy. You can get the kids, but you have to be willing to recruit nationally. You have to broaden your horizon to find out where the kids are that fit your criteria. In the NFL, you usually have a chance to get only one number one draft choice a year. In college, it is realistic to expect that you can get ten of the best players in the country. With a little luck, you can get twenty-five.

Unlike the pros, you don't have a chance to pick them. You offer them a scholarship and they pick you. With almost every kid to whom you make an offer, we're just one of a whole bunch. How many college programs wouldn't have wanted Reggie Bush? They all wanted him. You just have to do a great job of recruiting and hope he picks your place.

It's important to identify the person who has the greatest influence on the kid's decision. You then try to get the opportunity to present the same thing to that person that you present to the kid; the difference is that you're talking to an adult. That person usually is a parent, but sometimes it's a coach.

I don't consider myself a salesman, which is how many other coaches approach recruiting. I consider myself a representative of Notre Dame. My job is to go out and represent what Notre Dame stands for. I think the fact that I am a Notre Dame graduate gives me an edge because I know the school firsthand.

The other thing I won't do—and it's one of my pet peeves—is negative recruiting, where you bad-mouth other schools competing for the same kid. When I go into a young man's house and talk to his parents and his coaches and his community leaders, I never mention another university, because I believe I have the best product. Why do I need to spend one second of time talking about the competitors?

I can't say the same for a large number of coaches from other schools who give kids all sorts of reasons why they shouldn't go to Notre Dame: "You're African American. What are you going to do in South Bend, Indiana? . . . The weather's no good; it's too cold in the winter. . . . You're not Catholic. . . . It's too tough academically."

Every time those issues come up with a recruit, I have him talk with the people who can address them appropriately. For example, Mike Haywood, my offensive coordinator, is an African American from Houston who played at Notre Dame. He's a great resource when someone asks questions that I can't answer. In '05 we had a defensive captain, Brandon Hoyte, who was an African American Jehovah's Witness from New Jersey. That kind of throws the you-have-to-be-Catholic-to-go-to-Notre Dame theory out the window.

If a recruit brings up our weather, I always respond with this question: "Do you want to play in the NFL?" Their answer is always "Yes." Then I go show them all of the sites in the NFL where it snows during the season.

"So I guess we should eliminate them as teams you would

want to play for if you go to the NFL," I say. "You're not playing in Buffalo, right? You're not playing in Green Bay. It doesn't look like you're going to the Giants or Jets. Throw out the Patriots. The Philadelphia Eagles? Throw them out too. You're not playing for the Steelers, Browns, or Bears, either."

All of a sudden, when they start hearing that, it opens their eyes. They say, "Yeah, I guess I didn't think that one all the way through."

All of these guys we recruit are very impressionable. They all think they're going to play in the NFL. That's why, when I'm on the road recruiting, I make sure to wear the fourth Super Bowl ring I won as a coach from the Patriots' victory over Philadelphia. I wear that one because it's the biggest. In fact, when I'm around recruits and they ask me a question, I'll hold the hand with the ring on it in front of my face as if I'm really thinking about the answer. What I'm actually doing is making sure they can see that giant ring with the glistening diamonds. If I can just get them to look at my hand instead of my face, I think I've got a good chance.

The kids we talk to about playing at Notre Dame all aspire to play on Sundays. In many cases, they have scholarship offers from as many as thirty other schools with Division I football programs. The question I ask every one of them, with their parents present, is, "If you got hurt today and could never play football again, of all of the schools that are offering you scholarships, which one would you like to have a degree from to go out into the real world and support yourself?"

At least nine out of ten of them say, "Notre Dame."

You have to find the ones that are not hypocritical about academics, who want a meaningful degree that they can use when they're done playing football, whether it's at the end of their college career or at the end of their pro career. That's important because if the kids don't care about school, Notre Dame is not the easiest place for them to choose. There are a lot of choices they can make that are much easier than ours.

Fortunately, the kids who want to come to Notre Dame are usually the ones who believe academics are important, who feel they're getting an Ivy League education while being part of a Division I football program. That's the type of kid we're looking for. In 2005, for every four kids who made official visits to attend Notre Dame on football scholarships, three said yes. That means that 75 percent of the kids who visited us committed to Notre Dame.

One trip to the guidance office could nix a guy for me in a second. I don't play with them. If school's not important, I'm out of there. In 2006, I was visiting a kid who played linebacker for a school in Pennsylvania. He knew I was going to be at the school at eight o'clock in the morning. I arrived at the school with one of my assistant coaches before eight o'clock. The kid showed up at eight thirty. He told his coach he overslept. That didn't send a very good message. Then I walked into the guidance office and found out that the kid had missed seventeen days of school so far during that semester because he was off visiting colleges and just blowing off school, and his grades were plummeting.

At about eight thirty-five, we walked out of that school. I called the office and said, "Take him off the board. We're no longer interested in this guy."

I'VE BEEN PART of a team of coaches that has gone into many places where the team was crummy, and in a short time we made it competitive. We did it in New England. We did it with the Jets.

We did it in New England again. Now, after being an assistant my whole life in the NFL, I'm the head coach at one of the most storied programs in sports.

We have a program with integrity. We have one voice, we have discipline, we intend to outwork everyone we play against, and we're not going to accept anyone who is not going to be on board. It doesn't make any difference how good he is.

In my first season at Notre Dame we won nine games and lost three. The year before, the team had won six and lost six. The year before that, they won five and lost seven. Most Notre Dame people were delighted that we went 9–3 in 2005. I was miserable about it. I couldn't listen to one more alum coming up to me and saying, "Good year!"

My response usually went: "Nine-and-three is a good year? That means there were three times where we went out there and I messed it up somehow."

After the '05 season, I had a giant banner made that said: "9–3 IS NOT GOOD ENOUGH." It hangs from the balcony in our weight room. It's a daily reminder to our players that each year, the bar is set higher. Our guys have had a little sense of what winning tastes like. Now I want them to take it to another level.

When you're setting goals, 9–3 isn't something you shoot for. What you shoot for is 12–0 and a national championship. In the NFL, the only goal is to win the Super Bowl. In college football, it's the national championship.

Each of the four Super Bowl rings I have is a symbol that I was part of the best of the best. Why would you set your goals any lower than that? Either you beat every team on your schedule or you're not successful. There's no middle of the road.

I'm shooting for a national championship every year. Is that

realistic? Probably not to anyone except me. I'm probably halluci-
nating to have such a vision, but that's going to be my goal every
single year.

Whenever my team goes out there, I expect to win. I don't care
who we're playing. I don't care where we're playing. I don't care
what the weather's like. I don't care what their record is.

I don't believe in excuses.

Acknowledgments

We wish to recognize the following people for their help in the production of this book:

Special thanks to Mauro DiPreta, for his vision, guidance, masterful editing, and constant encouragement; Joelle Yudin, for keeping the production on schedule and for pulling the whole process together; Tim McDonnell, for always being there to provide whatever was needed to complete the project and for tending to every last detail; Bob and Lynn LaMonte, for believing that there was a story that needed to be told and for getting the project off the ground; and Basil Kane, literary agent extraordinaire, for being his usual supportive self.

We also would like to express our gratitude to Jim Boothby, Marie Coukos, Steve Fink, Pat Hanlon, John Heisler, Stacey James,

Acknowledgments

Chad Klunder, Bert Lane, Doug Miller, Mike Mone, Casey O'Connell, Dave Perry, Jerry Pinkus, Jared Puffer, Debbie Weis, and Maura Weis.

Additionally, we'd like to thank Rhonda, Kristen, and Lindsay Carucci for their patience, understanding, and support.